PRESENCE OVER PAIN

HOW GOD'S PRESENCE IS THE ANSWER TO OUR PAIN

BY DOUG RUMBOLD

TRILOGY

Presence Over Pain: How God's Presence is the Answer to Our Pain

Trilogy Christian Publishers A Wholly Owned Subsidary of Trinity Broadcasting Network

2442 Michelle Drive Tustin, CA 92780

Cover design by: Julie Morr

For information about special discounts for bulk purchases, please contact Trilogy Christian Publishing.

Trilogy Disclaimer: The views and content expressed in this book are those of the author and may not necessarily reflect the views and doctrine of Trilogy Christian Publishing or the Trinity Broadcasting Network.

Manufactured in the United States of America

10 9 8 7 6 5 4 3 2 1

Library of Congress Cataloging-in-Publication Data is available.

ISBN: 979-8-88738-296-8

E-ISBN: 979-8-88738-297-5

DEDICATION TO JESSICA

To the one who has taught me that God's presence presides over pain in unexpected and glorious ways. Our marriage is stronger, in part, because of your unwavering commitment to this principle— *Christ in you the hope of Glory.*

Acknowledgments

To my parents, my own children, my in-laws, dear friends, and many in my church family: you have walked through the trials with me that have made up much of the content for this book.

"God must love the blues. There's a whole book in the Bible called Lamentations. The largest swath of Psalms are the laments. And don't forget the book of Job. God seems okay with suffering. Us? Not so much. Yet, suffering is a required course on the syllabus of following Jesus. The writer of Hebrews says this about Jesus and suffering: 'Though he were a Son, yet learned he obedience by the things which he suffered' (Hebrews 5:8). If Jesus learned through suffering, how much more is there for us to learn? Currently, we live in a Christian culture that embraces the happy parts of the Gospel (like heaven) but not so much the promised pain, suffering, and lamenting that come to all who aspire to follow Jesus. In this book, my friend, Doug Rumbold, dares to wrestle with the vexatious topic of suffering. As you will see, he and his wife, Jess, are no strangers to suffering. The cliché 'God will never give you more than you can handle' is about to be challenged. And yes, there is redemption. So, keep turning the pages. This book will point you to hope, whose name is Jesus. And Jesus said, 'I have told you these things, so that in me you may have peace. In this world you will have trouble. But take heart! I have overcome the world' (John 16:33)."

—Bill Allison,
Executive Director of Cadre Missionaries

"This book emerges from the heart of one that has experienced the anguish and confusion of loss and suffering. Doug takes us on a journey through the rugged terrain of suffering and provides not platitudes but a humble window into how God meets and sustains us in the most painful seasons. It will do your soul good. Read!"

—Craig Mercer, Counselor, Speaker,
Blogger at Twelve Stones Counseling Ministry

Table of Contents

FOREWORD

I first met Doug Rumbold many years ago when he was a high school student. I was the Chair of a Youth Ministry degree program at a small midwest Christian university. Doug's brother Ed was a student in that program.

I made it a point to engage my students inside and outside the classroom in mentoring relationships. I believed and taught that 80 percent of the education happened more in the context of relationship than it did in a lecture.

It was natural to have students in our home, come alongside them at the university events, and craft ministry experiences with them. I recall one weekend when a number of my students were traveling to Ed Rumbold's family farm about three hours from the university. I was asked to join, and I agreed. The Rumbolds were very gracious hosts providing food and more fun than ever expected. It was this weekend that I met Doug along with the rest of the Rumbold clan. Little did I know that Doug would soon be a freshman sitting in my classroom not long after.

I recall getting a disturbing phone call one night during Doug's freshman year. Tragedy had struck the Rumbold family when their youngest son Ben, walking along a country road near their home, was fatally struck when an auto came over a ridge.

This was the first time that I would have to meet one of my students who I loved and cared for, work through grief, pain, and suffering. This event rocked our community which rallied around Ed, Doug, and their family.

We all experience grief and pain. It is part of the human condition, but when a parent loses a child or a sibling loses a young sibling close in age, the trauma is accentuated because it is the least expected form of loss. Doug and Ben were close in age, and I knew this would be very difficult for him.

It was amazing to watch this family overcome the tragedy. Their love for each other, faith in Jesus, strong community, and resilient spirit brought them through. That didn't mean that the pain went away; it just provided a way to cope with and understand the grief and sorrow.

Over the years, Doug, his brother Ed, and the entire Rumbold family became very dear to me. I had the privilege of officiating Doug and Ed's weddings to amazing women, watching their families grow, and dealing with difficulties from the pain of illness to the loss of a parent.

Doug grew to be a great man who has helped many others through trauma, grief, and pain. He writes from knowledge and experience. It's a privilege for me to write the forward to this book written by one of my former students, protégée, and friend. Doug's words will bring healing and hope to any reader who suffers pain and loss.

—Steve Gerali,
D.Phil., D.Litt.

INTRODUCTION

I was a nineteen-year-old freshman in college when I received a call that my youngest brother had been struck by a car while on a walk with his friend about a mile from our home. We immediately rushed home to attend to him in the hospital as he was placed on life support for the benefit of the three of us, my siblings and I, who were three hours away from home. What transpired over the next few days and weeks were some of the hardest and darkest days I had walked through in my young life. I was always fascinated with how we try to process and reconcile suffering. The fascination to tinker with the idea abruptly shifted from mental meandering to experiential angst that fateful day. Yet one moment is burned into my mind, still choking my breathing and clouding my eyes even now.

It was his bedside. Though he was effectively dead at the site of the accident, a machine made it possible for him to have artificial breathing. I remember standing next to the bed and watching his lifeless body heaving up and down with the purr of an electric motor in the background. *I couldn't bring myself to touch his body.* The monitors indicated that his brain activity was that of a deceased person while the air that was pumped in and out gave the impression that, at any moment, he could rise and greet us. In the immediate aftermath of his passing, this is what haunted me the most; *the loneliness of it all.* At the greatest moment of suffering I had experienced to that point, coupled with watching my parents and family, I was struck by how abandoned or alone it felt to me. As my father pulled the power cord from the wall of the life support machine, I recall literally wedging myself behind it and wanting no one near but at the same time crying out inside for *a touch*. The problem was, in that moment, I only wanted people who *knew* and *understood* to be near me.

So, what was I grasping for? Would not a touch from someone who knew and understood be acceptable, even normal? A word of encouragement expressing shared sorrow surely would have helped. The explanation many seek in suffering is one that is meant to absorb the pain, make it so that each passing day carries with it a little less weight than the one before. We strive. We want to understand. If I knew *why* he died OR *what* the reason behind his passing was, then I would be more able to cope. Now that is an interesting conclusion, isn't it? As I look back, the meaning I was trying to make of my brother's passing extended even into my unconscious state for I had the same recurring dream (nightmare) for seven consecutive years each time I laid my head on the pillow. Knowledge after the fact does little to alleviate the depth of heartache one is experiencing presently. The young boy who touches the hot stove only to find he left part of his flesh on the burner will likely benefit little from an *immediate* rebuke about how burners are hot and shouldn't be touched. It is the comfort of his mom or dad who tenderly holds and gently speaks with the afflicted one that *really matters*. There is a time for instruction, just not right then.

At the end of the day, information can provide only some comfort but not The Comfort.

The presence of God, only His nearness in our lives provides for such comfort. The Apostle Paul understood this reality. In 2 Corinthians 1:3–11, we see a picture of how the comfort of God given by His Holy Spirit, made possible through Jesus Christ's death and resurrection doesn't remove sorrow or suffering, but it does sweeten it.

> Blessed be the God and Father of our Lord Jesus Christ, the Father of mercies and God of all comfort, who comforts us in all our affliction, so that we may be able to comfort those who are in any affliction, with the comfort with which we ourselves are comforted by God. For as we share abundantly in Christ's sufferings, so through Christ we share abundantly in comfort too. If we are afflicted, it is for your comfort and salvation; and if we are comforted, it is for your comfort, which you experience when you patiently endure the same sufferings that we suffer. Our hope for you is unshaken, for we know that as you share in our sufferings, you will also share in our comfort.

As Paul describes it, our experience of hardship actually increases our affection for Jesus, clarifies our calling, and fixes our hope where it belongs, causing us to be able to provide comfort for others. How can this be?

This is a book about suffering. You probably gathered as much by now. I am not sure how else to say this, but there are thousands of books on the topic. A quick internet search will yield everything from "how to suffer well, godly grieving, and why would a loving God allow (you name it)" to issues on anger in prolonged trial and how to quickly exit the pain you may find yourself in. I can safely say I am not planning on revealing anything which has not been covered in the last two millennia on the topic. In this way I will stay true to the logic of scripture, there truly is nothing new under the sun (Ecclesiastes 1:9). I am not that wise or insightful.

I am sure the reader of this may be wondering, *"Well, that sure is an odd way to start an introduction to a book you want me to read.*

Perhaps the honest approach and stark assessment of what your book will not be is not the best marketing strategy." They would be right. My goal is not to inform you how poorly you are suffering, as though it is some sport one can train for and demonstrate proficiency at, though what we discuss will prepare you for *that* day when it comes, and *come it will.* God is more vast and comprehensive in knowledge and the exercise of His sovereign love than I could possibly imagine; therefore, it is an arrogant person who claims to have the complete answer for a person's particular suffering.

I believe, and will explain in the pages to follow, that while there may be a litany of reasons for suffering, Scripture seems to break it down to about three. There is the suffering that *God permits.* Quickly open your Bible, and you will see in the book of Job a prime example of this. He is doing nothing which "deserves" punishment or suffering, yet when the Adversary comes to God, He inexplicably offers up Job as sort of a guinea pig on whom he can test the limits of human anguish. Truly it is gruesome and hard to read. What can be learned in this form of suffering? How is God near in this setting? Through Scripture and story, we will address the *suffering God permits.*

Secondly, there is the suffering that *I cause.* In 2 Samuel 11–12, there is a story of King David, who should be tending to his kingdom and at war protecting it, yet the narrative finds him on the roof of his home gawking at a bathing woman who is not his wife. Everything, and I mean E-V-E-R-Y-T-H-I-N-G, unravels from there. It takes a pretty obvious fictional story from a trusted prophet to get David's attention; however, many of the consequences he is warned of come to pass *post* repentance. What can be learned from this form of suffering? How is God near in this setting? Through Scripture and story, we will address the *suffering I cause.*

Finally, there is the suffering that my faith provokes. In Acts 5, we read a story of how a high priest and the ruling religious elite had wounded pride which led to the arrest and imprisonment of the Apostles. The church was growing like crazy, and many miraculous things were being done by the Apostles, but the high priest couldn't stomach it all. The Apostles are arrested, but soon an angel of the Lord opens the doors. The following day guards and assistants are perplexed because the same Apostles are now in the public square proclaiming Christ, *again*. Infuriated, they bring them in, question them, severely beat them, and tell them to "shut up." They instead *rejoiced*. What can be learned in this form of suffering? How is God near in this setting? Through Scripture and story, we will address the *suffering my faith provokes*.

If one were to read Genesis 1 and 2, they would find a picture of the wonder and glory of creation; God is totally pleased with all He has made. All is as all should be, and from that vantage point, it is a terrible cliff the reader is pushed over when he or she continues on to chapter 3. It is here that we discover Adam and Eve making choices that mar the rest of mankind indelibly forever. Without getting into a blame game of who did what first, we can easily arrive at the conclusion humanity "*done messed up.*" Adam and Eve sinned, they missed the mark and so introduced suffering into the world. As a result, the perfection and intimacy first available at creation through the very *near* presence of God was forfeited because of a selfish lust for power, control, and position (again, read Genesis 3). The reader is compelled onward as the unfolding narrative of Scripture illustrates God's initiative toward His wayward children. Eventually, we come to Revelation 21–22, where the promise of God is *to wipe every tear from every eye*, make all things new, to eliminate mourning, crying, and pain—all punctuated by the very words of Jesus "I am coming soon" repeated three times in Revelation 22.

It is here John sees in a vision from God that all His promises for restoration and redemption are taking place, yet even while writing Revelation, he is in exile on Patmos (a Grecian Island off the east coast of modern Turkey). This is the same John who, about 10-15 years earlier, had penned the Gospel of John. In John 16:33, we learn that Jesus spoke words of comfort for a reason, "*I have said these things to you, that in me you may have peace. In the world you will have tribulation. But take heart; I have overcome the world*" (ESV).[1] So John is on the island, alone, writing about every tear being wiped from every eye without the advantage of it actually happening and likely recalling the *other* promise, "…in the world, you will have tribulation." There must have been a bridge of sorts to connect the present reality with the future hope for John. The bridge, I believe is His *nearness, His very presence.* Will you journey with me as we seek to believe together the words of Psalm 16:11 "…in your presence, there is fullness of joy"? (ESV)[2]

One word for the context. The particular path that God has us on as a family has leaned more heavily into the suffering that God permits, and I will find it impossible to avoid sharing some of our journeys. My hope is not to make us examples, good or bad, rather it is to flip the spotlight onto Jesus Christ—our enduring hope. Finally, there is a vast array of words used to describe suffering, and I will use them somewhat interchangeably throughout. Words like suffering, pain, affliction, hardship, trial, difficulty, and adversity—be on the lookout for those.

Chapter 1—The Dangerous Prayer

Beginnings...

There was a time years ago when I was scared to death. You know the fear that I speak of. It is the cold sweat, something under every rock and behind every door type of fear. I had just spent the better part of an hour in a Sunday school classroom in the basement of the church of my youth. The teacher, a middle-aged woman with a deep love for Christ, had just shared the Gospel with us. The picture of life lived *with Christ* was compelling, but the obstacle I faced was the fear of punishment. The consequence which awaited the unrepentant sinner drove me to tears. I had not yet understood that "perfect love drives out fear" (ESV).[3] I was paralyzed in that classroom with genuine concern for my eternal state. Having arrived home from church, I was found by my mother out of sorts. After a battery of questions, she discovered I was not "...found in Him, not having a righteousness of my own that comes from the law, but that which comes through faith in Christ, the righteousness from God that depends on faith" (Philippians 3:9, ESV) as the Apostle Paul so eloquently put it (ESV).[4] Plainly stated, I was not a disciple of Jesus.

The remedy for my problem was an event that began a process, one I am still experiencing today. Allow me to explain. In Romans 10, we learn that if one confesses "with their mouth that Jesus is Lord and believe(s) in your heart that God raised him from the dead, you will be saved" (Romans 10:9, ESV).[5] I was led in a prayer that followed the form in that verse and was "saved." There, done, I had been *saved*, that should be enough, right? Wherever it was that one stores their "Admit One" ticket to heaven for the years until their death, I had mine now. Certainly, God was not concerned with me after that.

Never have I disagreed more with the "one and done, fire insurance, got my ticket" view of salvation than I do currently!

Theologically speaking, it is the process of *being saved* that so few of us, myself included, really understand or *yearn* for. After the lights have faded and the excitement of the event has worn off, where are we really? Were we more enamored with the comfort that saying a prayer of salvation gave us or could there be more? The companion concept that one often hears with *salvation* is the word "sanctification." Martin Manser defines it like this:

The process of becoming consecrated to God, which is an integral aspect of being a member of the people of God. This process of being made holy through the work of the Holy Spirit ultimately rests upon the sacrificial death of Jesus Christ...[6]

Manser connects on a deeper level with what "church folk" think or know about sanctification. We become set apart *to God.* The Holy Spirit does this in us as we go through all of life; the hardships, the valleys, the mountaintops, and the meadows of ease. Still, what does it mean on a more down-to-earth level? It has been said before: sanctification is progressively becoming more like Jesus. If we are created in the image of God (Genesis 1:26–27) and Jesus is God in the flesh (John 1:14 and Hebrews 1:1–3), then you and I must take our cues from the life of Jesus when it comes to "becoming more like Him."

It is at this point that I want to exercise caution. The makeup of my heart requires His special and personal care. The same is true with you. God has His hand upon you even as you read this. Even if you are reading this without the advantage of having a personal relationship with God through Christ, He is already using this work in *your story*. I will not presume to know how God will work to make you look more like Jesus. However, I do know that cannot happen until one surrenders to Him, confesses their sin and His Lordship over their lives, and seeks to live according to His will as revealed in the Bible.

A basic way to understand sanctification as a process revealed over time is to watch a parent and their child. I have two sons, for whom I am very thankful. At their birth, both of them didn't look a whole lot like me. Instead, they were cute, chubby, and cuddly; the trifecta, if you will. However, as my middle son ages, we see how he resembles me in various ways that have become more pronounced over the years. On the other hand, my youngest son mimics certain traits of his mother more than he does me. As these good characteristics become more evident, there is considerable time poured into the development and motivation behind them in the hope that God is honored and others are blessed through them. We accomplish this through various means such as teachable moments, discipline, explanation of consequence for sin, family chores, consistent time in the Bible together, prayer, and walking with them through hard things, just to name a few.

Do you believe that God works in a similar fashion? He put good in us by simply creating us in His image. Your value and vision in life ARE God-deposited, not self-initiated or self-sustained. This should be incredibly freeing, "I am valued by God *no matter what.*" God desires that we come to look more and more like His Son, and to get us there, He uses whatever means necessary. The matter for you and me must be settled straight away in our walk with Jesus: "*Do I really want to resemble Him, and if I do, am I okay with how God chooses to get me there?*"

The Prayer Which Requires a Seatbelt

We are not God. When we pray, He does not show us every little thing He is up to. It is designed this way so that we can have a clear view of one thing, HIM! Also, we are called to a life of faith. "Faith is the assurance of things hoped for, the conviction of things not seen."[7] The reality is that I can no more exercise control in my own life and manufacture outcomes than I can tell the sun to rise or set, leading me to trust God as sovereign, at least in my mind. So we pray with great sincerity, *"Lord, make me more like your Son, **whatever** it takes."* This is a dangerous prayer.

The prayer offered here, without the advantage of knowing the future, may soon find itself being walked back. "Excuse me, Lord, I was not certain what was included when I prayed that prayer. I'd like it if you could simply send me a bit of a road map that laid out some of the pitfalls, triumphs, and overall range of emotions I may experience on the way to you, making me look more like your Son." Sound familiar? Have you ever been there? Questions arise, which cast God's love into the realm of the unsure. *Certainly, if he loved me he would not allow this unbelievable difficulty to have emerged in my life.*

Therein lies the irony. From the rooftops, we would proclaim the Lord's kindness to us in Christ Jesus, and even extol the virtue of His loving care in all things. However, what I find to be slightly double-standard(ish) of myself at times is that I love God's power and control *in theory*, I'm just not so sure about how it gets worked out. Pain is not a welcome guest, nor is trial or difficulty in any form. Speaking practically and honestly, I try to avoid them for the most part. I'd venture a guess you may be the same.

I look around me to see those who are convinced that God loves them, and they live like it. The search for a common denominator begins, and it is not long until I discover that suffering or affliction are the catalysts. Those having a depth of maturity worth emulating are often the ones who speak of how they *know God* because of their suffering or in their suffering. Listen to the Apostle Paul writing while in chains for his faith:

> But whatever gain I had, I counted as loss *for the sake of Christ.* Indeed, I count everything as loss because of the *surpassing worth of knowing Christ* Jesus my Lord. For His sake, I have suffered the loss of all things and count them as rubbish, in order that I may gain Christ.
>
> Philippians 3:7–8 (ESV, italics mine)

Additionally, the presence of the Lord is not a theoretical construct or an abstract principle read about in a text book; His *nearness* is known, tangible, and reliable. To Paul, this meant nothing compared to knowing Christ. Really? Nothing? If I am being honest, this is not always the case with me. Perhaps you can relate and are a fellow "white-knuckler," desiring to have a mix of faith in God and control over your own life and circumstances. This is where Scripture comes to the rescue.

Joy Weaponized

First Peter is a fascinating book that combines deep suffering and future hope bridged by the very presence of God. It is written to Christians scattered throughout modern-day Turkey, roughly a land area the size of Texas. The setting is about thirty years after Christ, and already persecution, the suffering my faith provokes, is taking place and has the potential to discourage. For example, the emperor Nero engaged in the heinous treatment of Christians in Rome that included wrapping them in dead animal skins, dipping them in tar, and lighting them on fire in order to illuminate his gardens at night.[8] Though this was not something that occurred throughout the entire Roman empire, the Christians reading the letter Peter sent were often disowned by their families and exiled for their faith. How these young believers viewed their trials had the potential to wreck their faith or shape their hope, and Peter knew it.

In one of the most poignant and powerful passages on suffering and joy, Peter speaks of our *living hope* (1 Peter 1:3–9):

> **Blessed be the God and Father of our Lord Jesus Christ! According to his great mercy, he has caused us to be born again to a living hope through the resurrection of Jesus Christ from the dead, to an inheritance that is imperishable, undefiled, and unfading, kept in heaven for you, who by God's power are being guarded through faith for a salvation ready to be revealed in the last time. In this you rejoice, though now for a little while, if necessary, you have been grieved by various trials, so that the tested genuineness of your faith—more precious than gold that perishes though it is tested by fire—may be found to result in praise and glory and honor at the revelation of Jesus Christ. Though you have not seen him, you love him. Though you do not now see him, you believe in him and rejoice with joy that is inexpressible and filled with glory, obtaining the outcome of your faith, the salvation of your souls.**

He does this to provide a foundation for those experiencing incredible difficulties and remind them how they, and we, should look at our hardships. God's *mercy* and our *living hope* are tied to the *resurrection of Jesus* (v. 3). The inheritance we have is *imperishable, undefiled, and unfading*; completely guarded by God (v. 4–5). The combination leads to rejoicing though present trials still exist (v. 6). It is then revealed that genuine faith is more valuable than gold that is *tested by fire*. So the faith that is tested by fire (hardships, trials, suffering) proves genuine, and this leads to the *joy that is inexpressible*. I want that, don't you?

> ### Joy, in the sense that Peter is describing, has the feel of a weapon where I can fight back against the enemies of discouragement, fear, anxiety, and apathy.

He's describing a weapon I desperately need; I'm hoping you do as well. It is not joy in the lower-case sense like that of a good cup of coffee or flowers on your desk unannounced at work. Rich, contextual, durable, inexpressible joy is the substance of his declaration.

The goldsmith reading the letter of 1 Peter would have immediately resonated with the example given. For gold to be formed into something useful it has to be cast into a mold of sorts. Picture an earring or a piece of jewelry that has a particular shape. For that to occur, it has to be melted at 1,900° Fahrenheit. Once this is done all impurities rise to the top and are skimmed off. The goldsmith is able to see his reflection in the gold as it is now mirror-like.[9] Now we are getting somewhere.

There was a time when fear gripped me because I was ignorant of how my sin separated me from a just but loving and gracious God. Thankfully, someone loved me enough to share that a relationship with God through Jesus Christ was the answer. Enthusiastically I embarked on a journey that is still being traveled today. This journey, however, does come with some challenges as God uses suffering or affliction to make me look more like Jesus. I am under the assumption that I am writing to someone who has a similar conviction. Perhaps you are asking some questions too. Questions that I have and still ask as well.

The refining nature of my trials and the resulting joy has been the realization that greatly altered how I view suffering, particularly the suffering that God permits. How I arrived at this realization will set the stage for our journey toward understanding how his presence presides over my pain.

CHAPTER 2—SETTING THE STAGE

Everything Was Normal

A few years ago, we never obsessed over this concept of "normal." However, Covid has taught us that our desire for "normal" is anything that contains predictability and freedom of choice. In this case, I will speak on a "professional" or "career" level. Each person reading this has a "normal" day or activity that would fit well within what your profession is, whether that be a domestic engineer (stay-at-home mom), a laborer, or an executive. At the time this story took place, I had the joy of being a youth pastor at a loving family church in a small community right in the middle of the state of Illinois. If you are going the speed limit and you don't hit any lights, *wait there are no lights*, one can easily pass through the center of Tremont in less than ninety seconds. Normal for my wife and I would have been high school students in and out of our home for discussions, prayer, Bible study, and just fun. December 29, 2010, was just such a night, it was normal.

The semester was at a break, and many students had not gone to an annual youth retreat which was hosted in Ohio. To get to know the remaining students and just have some fun, we had a movie night scheduled. *Despicable Me* was the movie, snacks were provided, and many students showed up. Our basement at the time was not equipped to handle thirty-five teens, but it often did, and this night was no exception. Everything went as it should except for the little nagging thought in the back of my mind.

Back up a couple of hours in the day, and you would find my daughter Jada (five at the time) and me at the local medical clinic with a loving doctor from our church providing a physical for her to be enrolled in school. Jessica, my wife, was nearing full term with our third baby and was having complications, which made the current home-school option untenable. We had prayed and reasoned that it would be best to just send her to public school for the semester and see where we were once summer arrived. Providence is the protective care of God.[10] Keep that in mind.

Everything for the physical went great. Jada had met or exceeded all the curves and was really in great health. She lay on her back for the doctor to examine her abdominal cavity and just make sure all the organs were as they should be. Routine. His face darkened a bit as he felt around the lower abdomen. He looked me in the eye and said, "I just can't reconcile this in my thinking; Jada is so healthy in every other aspect. However, I don't want to just let it go, I am going to have you get an ultrasound tomorrow just to clear up any doubt." I was not too worried, but one wonders. This was the nagging thought even into the evening when the students began to arrive.

The next morning our lovely daughter was subjected to a number of different scans and tests beginning at 9:00 in the morning. The culmination came at about 6:30 p.m. in a quaint little office in downtown Peoria, Illinois. Walking through the eerily empty parking lot the air held a penetrating sting. The kind of sting you recognize from a midwestern winter; the wind isn't forceful, just enough to cause one's eyes to hurt or nose to run involuntarily. Once inside, our hearts gripped our chests like they never had before as we waited for the surgeon to walk in. Matter-of-factly she walks in and says, "I suppose you know why you are here." To which I responded, "No, actually, we have not received an answer yet about the meaning of any of these scans." To that point, we had been at an imaging facility, the hospital, and back home before her office. Her face fell, her eyes rise and lock my intent paternal stare, "I'm sorry to be the one that has to tell you this, but your daughter has a large tumor that we have determined is kidney cancer. The full ramifications will come once the pathology from the surgery is returned, but we are looking at early next week for a major surgery."

Words fail to describe in a sufficient manner how one feels in that moment but let me give it a shot. It's like you've been sucker punched in the gut, unable to catch your breath, your eyes become fountains dispensing salty fear and sadness, and everything that's happening somehow plays in slow-vivid-motion. Those emotions need no coaching, instinctively one knows what to do at that moment, and Jada did. She looked with wide, sad eyes at her mother and crawled up into her lap, resting her head on Jessica. Deep sobbing followed. Raw. This is the best and most fitting word to describe the moment. There are some reading this who have been there when the word "cancer" rolls reluctantly off the tongue of the attending physician, you know what I mean. Even now, somewhat removed from that horrific day, I taste the salt as tears run over the ridge of my mouth and moisten my lips.

Really? you think to yourself. *This will be our new normal?* So, we picked ourselves up from the chairs we had collapsed into just moments earlier and headed for the door. Walking to the van holding our sweet daughter in my arms and feeling the warmth of her tears as she buried her face in my neck is like a brand a horse receives whether he likes it or not. The sting of the cold air on that late December night, the experience after the diagnosis, and the phone calls on the way home, I won't, I refuse to forget. For they lay the foundation of the nearness of God that is born through trial, the blessing of affliction, if you will.

This is not the style of *blessing* one is accustomed to here in the US. When we consider blessing it is innately connected with financial, physical, or emotional well-being.

I believe the blessing God brings through affliction is primarily the shaping of the believing individual into the image of Jesus Christ.

Psalm 119:67 says it this way, *"Before I was afflicted I went astray, but now I keep your word."*[11] God always has been and will always be about the shaping of the saints through affliction.

The starting point is that our daughter was five years old when she was diagnosed with kidney cancer in the soft tissue on December 30. After a number of different tests and scans over that weekend, surgery was set for January 3 for the removal of what would later be described as a "football-sized tumor." In a sense, the journey to discovering God's presence over my pain started way back in that Sunday school classroom where fear reigned supreme so many years ago. To spare space and a host of lackluster stories, I will not begin there.

Chapter 3—The Blessing of Affliction

"They gave our Master a crown of thorns.
Why do we hope for a crown of roses?"

Martin Luther

Surgery

We approached the pre-operation room with a fair bit of trepidation, but then again, who wouldn't? However, we knew going in that it was going to be an arduous ordeal. So, Jessica and I wheel our only daughter back to the room and begin to tell her stories, anything to capture her attention and divert her mind from the task at hand. A line of different physicians come to see her, and you can see it building. You can see it in her eyes and witness it in her body language. The time is drawing near. Just moments before our daughter goes under the knife, she motions for me to come near. Her frail little body is covered in blankies and all the comforts we can afford physically while her heart is held up in prayer. As I get right next to her lips, she whispers in a barely audible voice, "Daddy, I don't want to cry," and then she begins to briefly shed a few tears.

Jess and I pray with her, remind her of the Lord's strength in her, and head off to the waiting room. It's hard to describe the range of emotions you experience as a parent when your child is undergoing a life-threatening surgery but suffice it to say all were present and accounted for. Every fifteen minutes the phone would ring with a brief update by the attending nurse to ease our troubled minds. For four and a half hours, we waited, prayed, worshipped, paced the floor, and cried.

We sat in a small conference room with some family while we waited for the surgeon to come to describe the surgery to us. Finally, she enters and calmly recounts the surgery and her findings to us. "Mr. and Mrs. Rumbold, this was one of the largest solid-state tumors I have ever removed. The reason the surgery took a little longer than expected was simply that we could not run the risk of puncturing the tumor in any way." With a few other words that are a blur now, she assured us that everything went according to plan and that Jada would be ready to see us in a short while. She woke from surgery and motioned for me to come near again. This time what she whispered warmed my heart, "I (*pant, pant, pant*), LOVE (*pant, pant*), YOU."

The Vision

The next morning as I sat reading my Bible and praying with Jada fast asleep and before the onslaught of support arrived, I had a vision of hope for my daughter and, for that matter, my whole family. First Peter 4:12–19 inspired this vision.

> Beloved, do not be surprised at the *fiery trial* when it comes upon you *to test you,* as though something strange were happening to you. *But rejoice insofar as you share Christ's sufferings,* that you may also *rejoice* and be *glad* when his glory is revealed. If you are insulted for the name of Christ, you are blessed, because the Spirit of glory and of God rests upon you. But let none of you suffer as a murderer or a thief or an evildoer or as a meddler. Yet *if anyone suffers as a Christian, let him not be ashamed,* but let

him glorify God in that name. For it is time
for judgment to begin at the household of
God; and if it begins with us, what will be
the outcome for those who do not obey
the gospel of God? And "If the righteous
is scarcely saved, what will become of the
ungodly and the sinner?" Therefore let
those who suffer according to God's will
entrust their souls to a faithful Creator while
doing good.[12]

1 Peter 4:12–19 (ESV, italics mine)

Why would Peter instruct this brand new church to count suffering as joy and not be surprised when trial comes? What can possibly be gained from walking headlong into hardship expecting glory to be revealed and entrusting ourselves to a *faithful* Creator?

It is easy to see how what they faced could derail them, for persecution that could result in death would shake even the most ardent Jesus-followers in His day. I would argue, however, that the same holds true for us today, regardless of whether we face persecution for our faith *or* hardship and suffering filtered through the hands of the loving Father. The default in times of trial may be to raise both our hands in anger at God for what appears to be inequitable treatment. Let's just be honest for a minute, our world is filled with "fair and equal" language, but the definition is not universal. However, if we are not careful, having both fists clenched toward the heavens teaches us a one-sided view of suffering and trial. That view, sadly, is all about me. We are encouraged in the Bible to express our anger or frustration with God (clenched fist), but let us not forget to keep the other hand open to receive the blessing that comes by way of affliction. If the Gospel was delivered with great pain to the Lord Jesus (emotionally, spiritually, and physically), why do I expect that

God would ever deliver the truth, depth, and beauty of the Gospel love he has for me without some level of affliction? Clearly, we should *not* expect anything less. In Hebrews 2:10, it says that Christ was made perfect through suffering. You and I are made to resemble Christ *MORE* as we suffer. However, it is not our chosen vehicle. Who wakes up each morning and says, *"Bring it on Lord, whatever the hardest, most deeply challenging circumstances and relationships are, I'm game."* No, to the contrary, we often pray in the opposite direction, *"Lord, don't let these things happen."*

I want you to literally pause as you read this and ask yourself the following question: when do *you* most deeply desire the presence of God? Is it in times of ease when things are great, money is in the bank, health is good and relationships are enjoyable? Or are you more keen to seek His presence when it feels like you are treading water in the middle of the ocean, scrambling to make sense of the utter senselessness of it all? In moments like these, I often reflect on a phrase my wife has coined in our home and with friends. When asked about the hardship she's lived through, and whether she would trade it, she inevitably replies,

> **"No. Suffering is terribly wonderful, and it makes me long for the presence of God like nothing else. All of it makes me desperate for Him."**

Those Who've Gone Before

In Romans 15:4, Paul reminds us that "whatever was written in former days (referring to everything in the Bible that predates his letter to the Christians in Rome) was written for our instruction, that through endurance and the encouragement of the Scriptures we might have hope"[13] (Romans 15:4, ESV). One does not have to be a biblical scholar in order to see that pictures abound throughout the Old Testament, pointing its reader to the reality that God's nearness always matters more to the one who *hungers* for it. In all honesty, this truth is something that can be taught over and over, but until someone experiences the hunger pangs which accompany desperation for God to move and meet them personally, theory trumps practice. It doesn't stop there either. In fact, we are so prone to wander that God literally fills the Bible with stories and imperatives to hunger and seek after Him in good times because it simply is not our natural bent to do so, but it lays a proper foundation.

Deuteronomy eight chronicles the concern of God for His people with regard to what will happen immediately after their deliverance from 430 years of systematic oppression. He says, "You shall remember the *whole way* the LORD your God has led you these forty years in the wilderness, that he might humble you, testing you to know what was in your heart…"[14] (Deuteronomy 8:2, ESV). What follows is the sincere concern of a loving Father that our hearts would be easily drawn away from Him with a nice house, fast car, and well-rounded 401k. The promise throughout Deuteronomy eight shows a Father's lavish love for His children. He *wants* what is best for them, but realizes the heart can easily be deceived. Without some level of trial functioning as a spiritual compass God's concern is this: "…then your heart be lifted up, and you (will) forget the LORD your God, who brought you out of the land of Egypt, out of the house of slavery…"[15] (Deuteronomy 8:14, ESV).

Ultimately, it is our suffering or affliction which cultivates a hunger for God; because His presence is what sustains us through it. This was as true of the Israelites in Deuteronomy 8:15-16 as it is of us today:

> "...who *led you* through the great and terrifying wilderness, with its fiery serpents and scorpions and thirsty ground where there was no water, who *brought you* water out of the flinty rock, who *fed you* in the wilderness with manna that your fathers did not know, that he might humble you and test you, *to do you good in the end*."[16]
>
> **Deuteronomy 8:15–16 (ESV)**

The reason suffering is not our chosen vehicle, so to speak, is that it lacks a GPS. Not long ago our home gained its first driver. My wife and I are on the opposite end of the spectrum here. I grew up in a home with many children and was the second youngest, so I was less worried as our daughter learned. My wife, however, was the oldest of two, and she had much more concern than I did, which has proved very helpful. However, I refuse to forget (because I documented it with a photo) my daughter's first question behind the wheel in that large parking lot; "So, when do I learn how to use the GPS on my phone?" Incredulously I locked eyes with her and said, "I'm sorry, dear, you won't get that lesson from me; my job is to make sure you know your way around a car and around town. GPS is good for long trips and places you don't know, but you won't be headed there." It's like that with hardship in our lives, isn't it? A GPS would allow us to know what bends, valleys, and potholes may lie ahead. However, a loving Father, who has never failed a promise (see Joshua 21:45), told the Israelites all they were experiencing was that He might "...*do you (them) good in the end*." What an incredible promise to link arms with! We are not left to figure this out or on some meaningless hamster wheel of hardship.

In the introduction, I posited three different modes of suffering. There is the suffering that *God permits* independent of my character or conduct. Job is a good example of this in the Old Testament. Then there is suffering *I cause* when I sin. As a trusted mentor once said, "Choose to sin, choose to suffer." King David serves as a picture of this hard reality. Finally, suffering is brought on by faith in God. In fact, the Apostle Paul once said, "*Indeed, all who desire to live a godly life in Christ Jesus will be persecuted...*"[17] In the past ten years, we have walked a journey that has had me confronting each of the various modes of suffering and what I believe about them on a personal level. The earnest desire of my heart is that you come to understand the presence of God *in and through* suffering, no matter its cause. This next chapter will chronicle the revelation of God to my heart about how suffering turned from self to a plea for His presence! Specifically, I will explain what I call "the three C's": Christ, Community, and Confession.

Chapter 4—Bridge Over Troubled Water

"Though the Lord gave you adversity for food and suffering for drink, *he will still be with you to teach you.* You will see your teacher with your own eyes."

Isaiah 30:20 (NLT)

I woke as the sun peeked through the eastern window under the blinds providing precious little of the coverage they were designed for. Another night in the hospital was spent in periodic fits of restless sleep on a couch too short and firm to be called a bed. I reluctantly rose and silently slipped out of the room so as not to wake my daughter. I found the waiting room and an uninspiring cup of coffee, but quality was not my concern, hot and caffeinated was. I made my way down to the playroom at the end of the children's wing and looked over the downtown area as it glowed amber in the first light of morning. My mind was like a hamster wheel running, always running. I contemplated my daughter's hardship, my middle son (who was two at the time) and all he must be thinking, my youngest son (who was born only a few days after my daughter's surgery), and his first experiences in this world. Finally, my mind was flooded with all my wife must be facing only recently removed from childbirth and caring for two boys.

I clutched my Bible, holding it tightly to my chest as I curled up in the chair. Desperately flipping pages seeking a comforting verse or passage to assuage the onset of intrusive thoughts. I set it down and began to simply jot down my concerns in prayer form. "Father,

I am not sure I can muster the courage this is going to take. I am deeply concerned…" and I trailed off. Fear of the unknown began to grip me. The options were limitless, yet none of them seemed consoling. Funny how our mind does that at times. Anxiety usually has a penchant for catastrophe. I needed comfort. I needed assurance of His loving protection. I needed Him *with* me! As I read, *"'I will never leave you nor forsake you.' So we can confidently say, 'The Lord is my helper; I will not fear; what can man do to me?'"* (Hebrews 13:5–6, ESV)[18] my heart gained some momentum. "So He's *here* and He hasn't forgotten about us? I guess that means I can approach Him with the concerns I have." No sooner had the thought crossed my mind did I notice the sun's warmth on my face and time slipping away. I had to get back to that room and her bedside before she awoke. Thinking I would definitely return and finish this silent dialogue, I just bookmarked my journal and grabbed my Bible.

On the way back to the room, I was already parsing through the implications of His presence over our pain. The scary thing facing me presently was the endurance this was going to require. "How would we get through?" I kept asking myself. As if I had uttered it out loud, I sensed the gentle but timely rebuke of God's still, small voice. It started with a subtly powerful reminder, "Since he did not spare even his own Son but gave him up for us all, won't he also give us everything else?" (Romans 8:32, NLT)[19] Jesus had experienced a trial beyond comparison with any the likes of humanity will ever see. He *willingly* bore the sin of everyone when He wasn't the culprit at all. What's more, He knew it was coming and trusted His Father to help Him endure. There was a momentary blip on the cross where Jesus uttered, "My God, my God, why have you forsaken me?" (Matthew 27:46, ESV).[20] Suddenly, the terrible and profoundly wonderful realization captured me; he endured being *forsaken* by God so that I never have to!

One of the goals of His suffering was to give ultimate purpose and meaning to mine.

Through His sacrifice, I get Him, in the here and now and for eternity!

If you have walked with the Lord at all through the challenges this life brings, you know there are times when he *has* your attention; this was just such a time. His voice continued, "What about the devastation the loss of your brother brought? Was I not in the midst of that untimely and grief-stricken season? Were not people brought into my eternal family as a result? Didn't you come out of your shell and begin to see the value of deep friendship as opposed to isolation and Lone-Ranger Christianity?"

I had to admit, He had a point. In the years following his passing, I had heard testimony after testimony of God bringing glory to Himself through the tragedy. His classmates, my collegiate friends, and our family; his death brought about so much good. Though I had not slept well and encountered nightmares regularly, I couldn't deny His powerful hand working in me a profound hunger for more of Him. It was in this season that I began to delve deeper into the heart of God through prayer and journaling. In addition, I recall a few friends and family members who simply refused to let me crawl into the guarded comfort of personal solitude and instead brought me into the light of vital relationships. Already the argument of how we'd make it through was losing its strength in light of the powerful yet gentle questions the Spirit of God was raising in objection.

I arrived back in the room to our daughter, still snoozing in the early light. Machines chirping in the background did their best to distract me, but my mind is a bit of a steel trap when it gets locked on something in particular. I settled into the uncomfortable quasi-bed I was growing accustomed to but sat upright in the corner near the window so that this little inner discussion might resume. Peering out over the cold concrete parking deck with the long shadows of morning growing more distinct, I mused, "Okay, so I will give You the fact that You were there through *it all* when it came to my little brother's passing. However, what will become of us as a family now? I mean, for the next eight to ten months we are splitting time. My wife is home with a confused and hurting toddler as well as a constantly needy newborn while I am lodging here caring for a youngster whose whole world is literally upside down and painful to boot." Only a few moments of silence weighed on me as I anticipated an answer. A noise from behind jarred me, and I was greeted by the sweetest eyes of our firstborn. Though gaunt and half-hearted her smile managed to pause the conversation in my mind.

The hospital room had a warm orange glow from the rising sun outside as the doctors came in to do their rounds. Question after question followed, and we were soon knee-deep in our new normal. "How was your evening, did she tolerate the last infusion of chemotherapy well, any issues with vomiting, is she hydrated properly, etc.?" In the back of my mind, I had intended to resume the dialogue, but if I am honest, I simply forgot. Lack of sleep will do that to you; rob you of your sanity and recollection altogether. Hours passed, more treatment was administered, and as evening approached, I decided I was going to drive home to grab a shower and change of clothes before bedtime.

I approached the car, which by desire of our precious patient, had to be parked on the seventh floor of the parking deck. I was happy to oblige each time we would return to the hospital for her treatment cycles by finding a spot on the highest floor so we could see the hustle and bustle below. The perspective it provided over the city of Peoria, Illinois, was indeed beautiful. On that particular evening, I quickly exited the parking structure because I wanted a proper meal with a good shower. I couldn't bring myself to turn on the radio, all the noise of the hospital had conditioned me for silence. Picking up speed, I merged with traffic and began to approach the Illinois River. The drone of my tires on the highway with the occasional hiccup of a seam in the concrete was almost rhythmic. My mind wandered to the words of Isaiah 43:2 "When you pass through the waters, I will be with you; and through the rivers, they shall not overwhelm you..." (Isaiah 43:2, ESV)[21] Then, the still, small voice spoke loud and clear. *"You're wondering how your family will make it through... Christ, community and confession."*

I continued driving and recalled the dialogue begun that morning I had previously forgotten. How kind of the Lord to return to it in the way He did, in the privacy of a moment with only Him and I. No beeping machines, no distractions of well-meaning visitors, no intrusions of resident physicians; just the silent hum of the highway coupled with the moving stream of head and tail lights. "Why Christ, community, and confession? What could those three words possibly mean?" With the cruise set, I simply began talking out loud to God in the car. Some would argue that's what happens when you begin to lose your mind. I've grown more fond of audible chats with my loving Father in recent years. Very tenderly the Holy Spirit began to remind me of earlier. "Of course," I thought, "*Christ* bore a suffering way worse than I could comprehend and endured being forsaken by His own Father, so I never have to be." I mulled this over for a bit, and it became clear that Jesus Christ had to suffer in order to deliver to you and me our only path to redemption. "Oh thank you, God! Your wisdom is incredible, and I can't comprehend it!" The Apostle Paul had discussed knowing Christ by sharing in His suffering (Philippians 3:7–11). You and I simply cannot grasp the wisdom of God in permitting suffering for His children. Paradoxically, it is how we are made to resemble Him.

Like a wave, stories from the *community* of believers around me when my brother passed were vividly displayed in my mind's eye. It was only a few hours earlier that I had been considering how others (both family and friends) surrounded me, and we journeyed together through the valley of the shadow of death to come out the other side! Again I found myself in awe, wonder, and praise driving down the highway. Nearly undone at His faithfulness, I began instinctively giving praise to those individuals who had been so instrumental through that season of grieving.

Finally, woven throughout the revelation of *Christ's* endurance and willingness to be forsaken, along with how He supplied the *community* around me for support was this concept of *confession*. I must admit, the first two words, upon further examination made sense while confession was a little harder to grasp. I pictured a courtroom scene in which the accused *confessed* his wrongdoing and received his just sentencing.

In a clarion moment that I can only attribute to the Lord, I began to consider how *a confessing* person was simply speaking in agreement with the charges leveled against him. The foundation of *speaking in agreement* was then applied to the truth and promises of scripture; "Of course, the unwavering confidence of *Christ*, the refrain of the *community* of believers around us, was all anchored to the penetrating and eternal words of God Himself!" The three words He gave worked in concert, if you will. Each adding a layer of rich and textured meaning to the suffering presently happening but all combining to communicate His very near presence *through* it all. I was beginning to see how the presence of God was and is the bridge over my troubled waters.

CHAPTER 5—WHAT THE WORLD

"Why do bad things happen to good people? *That only happened once and He volunteered."*

R. C. Sproul Jr.

The sun is just climbing over a distant horizon while the raspy whistle of an aging man is faintly audible. He is going about his morning routine, which he follows to make amends between God and his children after one of their opulent celebrations. Traditionally one would make a sacrifice for sin by offering an animal of value on an altar for their wrongdoing, something this father was intent on carrying out. The reasons for these parties are not fully understood, only that they are regular and licentious, eating and drinking to the heart's content. Cost is no issue either because the wealth of this man and his family is the stuff of legends. One can safely assume the frequency is also high because he has ten children. As a father, I empathize with the struggle about to unfold. Even though he is diligent and joyful about the work of preparing sacrifices to consecrate his children, his heart is inexorably bound up in their welfare. Any parent will attest the love they feel for someone they have borne or adopted is nearly unbreakable.

Job, the protagonist in this story, is a man from ancient times recorded in the book of the Bible that bears his name. He has prolific wealth and substantial influence. Greater still, it would appear, is his *godliness*. The book opens with the designation that he is "… blameless and upright, one who feared God and turned away from evil" (Job 1:1, ESV).[22] From this vantage point, the picture painted of Job is that he is one of the "good guys."

To be honest, as I read the account, I wrestle with some emotions. On the one hand, I like him and want to be known by God and others as he is. I mean, just pause and consider the powerful descriptors the author employs, *blameless, upright, fearing God, turning from evil.* He owns his stuff, has integrity, is motivated by an appropriate fear of the Almighty, and takes holiness seriously. Sounds like a dude I want to do life with. My sinister and darker self, however, is incredulous. "How in the world has this dunce stumbled into all this wealth and good fortune *(I'm just being real. If we can't be real, what are we doing here)*? What is his secret?" As you can see, the manifold wisdom of God is already on display because in the opening few lines of the book I am enraptured by the description of the main character and anticipate the story to follow.

The narrative commences with a scene depicting a council of sorts. God is clearly the ruler and ultimate authority as the *sons of God* and *Satan* (the Accuser or the Adversary—translation notes from the ESV Bible) present themselves before Him. It is helpful to note Satan himself and his minions are actually *fallen angels* (Isaiah 14, Ezekiel 28, Jude 6, Revelation 12:3–4, 9) who decided they wanted to usurp the power, authority, and glory associated with God Himself; making it safe to say that pride has been a problem even before humanity trolled the earth. We learn that the accuser and his comrades are essentially looking to wreak havoc wherever they can. Job is offered as someone who can stand whatever test may be lodged against him. In form-fitting fashion, this adversary snidely remarks, "Does Job fear God for no reason..." and insinuates his good fortune is the reason he clings to God. Permission, inexplicably, is granted for this ragtag bunch to annihilate all Job owns.

Efficient and total in carrying out the destruction they're permitted to enact, my heart reels as I read just ten short verses in Job chapter one. Job 1:13–22 (ESV)[23]:

> Now there was a day when his sons and daughters were eating and drinking wine in their oldest brother's house, and there came a messenger to Job and said, "The oxen were plowing and the donkeys feeding beside them, and the Sabeans fell upon them and took them and struck down the servants with the edge of the sword, and I alone have escaped to tell you." *While he was yet speaking*, there came another and said, "The fire of God fell from heaven and burned up the sheep and the servants and consumed them, and I alone have escaped to tell you." *While he was yet speaking*, there came another and said, "The Chaldeans formed three groups and made a raid on the camels and took them and struck down the servants with the edge of the sword, and I alone have escaped to tell you." *While he was yet speaking*, there came another and said, "Your sons and daughters were eating and drinking wine in their oldest brother's house, and behold, a great wind came across the wilderness and struck the four corners of the house, and it fell upon the young people, and they are dead, and I alone have escaped to tell you."
>
> Then Job arose and tore his robe and shaved his head and fell on the ground and

worshiped. And he said, "Naked I came from my mother's womb, and naked shall I return. The Lord gave, and the Lord has taken away; blessed be the name of the LORD."

In all this Job did not sin or charge God with wrong.

Job 1:13–22 (ESV, italics mine)

Everything is gone. Job's possessions and, more to the point, his children, have been snatched out from under him. Already questions are forming through the haze in my mind. Perhaps you are with me. When we first learn of Job, he is making sacrifices to appease his children's guilt before God for their over-the-top celebrations and libation. In one fail swoop, *his children are gone,* and with them, any hope that the regular sacrifices made on their behalf actually bought favor with God. He could not stop the tragedy. Job's response is not one I could have seen coming, he did not sin or blame God. Instead, he worshipped. Truly astonishing.

The desire to destroy and bring calamity still unquenched, the *sons of God* and *Satan* again present themselves before God and make a bold statement, "…all that a man has he will give for his life…" (Job 2:4, ESV).[24] It is easy to see what is going on here. These lunatics believe that if one has their health they have everything, but take his health, and he will have nothing to live for. Lunging for the jugular, quite literally, Satan makes the case to consume Job with physical suffering to see if his integrity and faith in God will hold the line. Again, without sufficient explanation, God allows this attack on Job's health but not unto death.

God's concession with this team of affliction A-listers is baffling and comfortless, to say the least. I have struggled with it since the time I first read it. In short order, his health is blown to pieces, and his physical pain is only magnified by his empathy-challenged wife as she begs him to curse God and die (story in Job 2:1–10). Job's deep and wise reply is sort of a gut punch to my whiny, "I've got a paper-cut" response whenever I have a cold: "Should we accept only good things from the hand of God and never anything bad?" So in all this, Job said nothing wrong" (Job 2:10, NLT).[25]

I've Got Questions

Stories of this magnitude tweak our justice bone. Someone, seemingly minding their own business, is thrust into the tumultuous waves of unexplained suffering by no fault of their own. What in the world is going on? How could a loving God allow… *You name it.* Think of someone you know. I encourage you right now to set down the book and identify someone who has experienced loss, physical discomfort, death of a loved one, financial ruin, broken relationships, and the list goes on. Now imagine what must be running through their mind. "Did I do something to deserve this? Why won't God heal me? How will I ever cope without the resources I once had? Is there anything that will relieve my pain?" Before we go any further, I want to address every heart reading this book. You are either heading into unexplained suffering, in the thick of it, or just exiting it. Wherever you find yourself, it is important to not write this off simply because it is not your present experience.

I know there are some who are waiting for me to provide a profoundly deep and relieving answer to the why of their suffering or that of a loved one. I empathize with the desire but will not offer something I do not believe God provides or I have. Risking the reality you could close the book and chuck it across the room now; I want to tell you there is a difference in the ultimate versus the immediate. Pain hurts. It alerts us something is wrong. When was the last time you noticed your toe or elbow when it was working properly? Never! The reality is, pain stops us in our tracks and demands a response. We would do well to pay close attention to it and address it, both physically and spiritually. We want, oftentimes, an immediate answer for what ails or befalls us. What God provides, however, is an *ultimate* answer with His *immanent* presence. Allow me to explain.

In John 9, Jesus and his disciples encounter an individual who is the victim of the prevailing notion of the day, *sickness or infirmity was always the result of someone's sin.* A man born blind is at the center of the controversy and Jesus' disciples ask, "Rabbi, who sinned, this man or his parents, that he was born blind?" Jesus answered, "It was not that this man sinned, or his parents, but that the works of God might be displayed in him" (John 9:2–3, ESV). Jesus, obliterating boundaries of societal construction as well as religious origin, intervenes and restores sight to the young man. As the exchange unfolds, this man realizes that only someone sent from God could have healed him. His parents, cowardly as they were, only affirm his blindness but keep their distance from Jesus and, by extension, their own son. The religious elite (Pharisees) pick the man and the healing apart, eventually casting the man out of their presence. *Unexplained suffering may often have isolating ripple effects*, which is a whole other book in itself.

Upon hearing the man's experience *after* being healed, Jesus seeks him out. He, the Savior and Messiah, sought out a no-name Jew, first for healing physically then for salvation! This speaks to the immediate and ultimate needs associated with hardship. The man's *immediate* need concerned physical sight. Jesus knew this and created a healing salve from his own spit and some dirt, placing it on his eyes. However, relief from his ailment physically was never the end game for Jesus, He is far too wise. Hearing he was now an outcast because of the work of healing and the religious institution's response, Jesus finds him and offers salvation. Jesus heard that they had cast him out, and having found him, He said, "Do you believe in the Son of Man?" He answered, "And who is he, sir, that I may believe in him?" Jesus said to him, "You have seen him, and it is he who is speaking to you." He said, "Lord, I believe," and he worshiped Him. Jesus said, "For judgment I came into this world, that those who do not see may see, and those who see may become blind" (John 9:35–39), which He gladly accepts. The *ultimate* answer for suffering had now been addressed, and his faith was placed in the *only one* who can save. Now our former blind man is on a trajectory of *becoming* like the one he is now able to *behold*. Did you catch that? Jesus *came* to him.

How Do We Get There?

Perhaps at this juncture, it's good to pause. When suffering comes upon you, and there is not a plausible or simple onramp to explain it, we may find ourselves reeling. In this moment then I believe it best to be clear regarding specifically *how* God's presence is the answer to your pain. You may recall that earlier on, I shared how Christ, community, and confession were spoken to me while traveling down the highway toward home after a particularly hard day of treatment for my daughter's cancer. With the cruise set on my 1998 Oldsmobile and my heart locked in and ready to hear from God, I was astounded by the simplicity of His reply. All the existential angst, tears, confusion, and pain were welling up within me. "Why? What did she do to deserve this? How long will this last?" and the list goes on. As clearly as I heard those three words as an answer to my questions, I also wanted to know how I would get there. Don't we all do that? We are meaning makers. Faith is the vehicle that brings His presence when suffering is inexplicable. I cried out early on for God to heal and help my daughter. He did! However, it was not immediate. Through Christ, community, and confession, my *faith* in God's loving care of me, despite the report of my perceptive faculties, was strengthened! Let's delve into each of these to see what God has for us.

Christ

On the eve of what would wind up being the most significant, magnanimous, and sacrificial act of human history—the Crucifixion—Jesus was understandably out of sorts. He had taken the disciples along with Him to Gethsemane after having shared their last meal together. Their minds, I am sure, are in a tug of war from the revelation that Judas would betray their Lord and Peter deny Him; the scene is fraught with tension. He instructs the disciples, "Sit here, while I go over there and pray" (Matthew 26:36, ESV). How Jesus enters into His greatest hour of suffering will be of unfathomable comfort to our hearts.

> Then Jesus went with them to a place called Gethsemane, and he said to his disciples, 'Sit here, while I go over there and pray. And taking with him Peter and the two sons of Zebedee, he began to be sorrowful and troubled. Then he said to them, 'My soul is very sorrowful, even to death; remain here, and watch with me.' And going a little farther he fell on his face and prayed, saying, 'My Father, if it be possible, let this cup pass from me; nevertheless, not as I will, but as you will.' And he came to the disciples and found them sleeping. And he said to Peter, 'So, could you not watch with me one hour? Watch and pray that you may not enter into temptation. The spirit indeed is willing, but the flesh is weak.' Again, for the second time, he went away and prayed, 'My Father,

if this cannot pass unless I drink it, your will
be done.' And again he came and found
them sleeping, for their eyes were heavy.
So, leaving them again, he went away and
prayed for the third time, saying the same
words again. Then he came to the disciples
and said to them, 'Sleep and take your
rest later on. See, the hour is at hand, and
the Son of Man is betrayed into the hands
of sinners. Rise, let us be going; see, my
betrayer is at hand.'

Matthew 26:36–46

Notice Jesus willingly enters, fully *trusts*, and vulnerably obeys the Father's very difficult directive to lay down His life. Here's how; when He enters the garden he gets three of the disciples to go in a bit further with Him (Matthew 26:37). The text says, "he began to be *sorrowful* and *troubled*" (Matthew 26:37, ESV). What is He doing? He's supposed to be strong, unflappable, and tough. Where are this white horse and flaming sword? He is the Lord, right?

There are two words I want to key in on before we transition to how Jesus incorporated community: *sorrowful* and *troubled*. Sorrow(ful) is used some twenty times in the New Testament and most simply means to be sad. One theologian captures it this way, "to be in heaviness."[26] Here is the Lord of all creation demonstrating a sadness that most would shy away from. Jesus was heavy-hearted, as the idiom goes, while he went about the business of securing our redemption.

Second, the text says he was "troubled," which simply means "to be in distress of mind."[27] The word itself is used about thirty times in the New Testament and connotes a mind/body connection with grief. To be *troubled*, one must be facing an event or situation that is incredibly hard, beyond the scope of their abilities, feels isolating, and causes questions of God's existence or involvement. Jesus checks all those boxes.

It is fascinating to consider what Jesus models here in His own suffering that is sovereignly permitted. The Biblical practice of lament is front and center as we witness Christ in deep anguish.

> ### *Lament is a faith-filled cry that trusts God yet expresses the trouble traversing the topography of life's hardships on the way to surrendering all to God.*

Ever been there? So overcome with discouragement and engulfed in suffering all you could do was cry out to God? The practice of lament itself acknowledges there is something deeply wrong and yet is tethered by an ultimate trust that God wins out. When expressed toward God it can be an act of worship; just read any number of Psalms to see it (I recommend Psalms 13 and 42). Though rocky and a bit like the always rough I-80 corridor south of Lake Michigan, it is a pathway nonetheless to the loving presence of God. Michael Card puts it this way, "Jesus understood that lament was the only true response of faith to the brokenness and fallenness of the world. It provides the only trustworthy bridge to God across the deep seismic quaking of our lives."[28] It appears lament is critical because each of us who name Jesus as Lord apprentice under His ways. It is filled with faith in the faithful God!

Community

In our passage, Jesus grabs three disciples (Peter, James, and John) and takes them right into the epicenter of suffering. Two observations bear pointing out which will have a direct influence on our own trials; remember you are either going in to, in the middle of, or coming out of something, so please don't skip to the next heading. *Jesus asked for prayer.* Wrap your head around that. Get a taste for that type of accessibility when it comes to *our Savior.* He admitted He was troubled, even to the point of death (Matthew 26:38), and asked them to pray. He knows the end of the story, yet He lets others in to intercede on His behalf. *Truth to life, who are you letting into your suffering and asking them to pray for you?*

The second move He makes is almost missed if you read too quickly. He takes them along to His place of pain, the garden. I call this the ministry of presence. In this fractured day and age in which we live, I have heard it said that we need the ministry of the ear more than the ministry of the mouth. A critical component of our walk with the Lord and with others is silent presence. Consider our story at the beginning of the chapter. Job was suffering beyond what any of us could possibly comprehend, and his friends showed up on the scene. The awkwardness of showing up to comfort the inconsolable is a task so monumental many of us wither internally just thinking about it. As I consider it all, I tremble a little because I know that out of love and deep concern many will fill the cavernous depths of another's trial with words too trite or cliché to be of any real value. I wish I could say this comes from a place of theory, but it does not as I have been both recipient and distributor of such words.

Job's friends hear of his great trials and we learn what they did first, "And they sat with him on the ground seven days and seven nights, and no one spoke a word to him, for they saw that his suffering was very great" (Job 2:13, ESV). Never mind the fact that if you keep reading, they actually open their mouth and remove all doubt concerning their ability to be comforters for him after this. The point, for our purposes here, stands that at the beginning, they offered the ministry of presence as Jesus' disciples did, who came with Him to the garden. *Truth to life, are you able to offer the ministry of presence to someone who is currently "sorrowful and troubled?" Or do you feel the need to speak?* It does not take an Ivy-league education or experiencing the same pain yourself. Often what God asks of us in a community is that we simply give *of* ourselves and be present with a sufferer. Consider the Prophet Isaiah as he spoke of Jesus, "He was... a man of sorrows and acquainted with grief" (Isaiah 53:3 ESV). In order to be "acquainted," there must be presence and contact.

Confession

Confession as a biblical concept is commonly thought of in a negative light; to admit one's wrongdoing or sin. That's a hard sell in today's world with all its "speak your truth," and "be your own person" propaganda. Who wants to really come under the authority of anyone, much less someone who preaches a way of life filled with sacrifice and humility. However, I propose we broaden our grasp of confession and in so doing recognize the power God has packed into the practice itself for our encouragement and hope, especially in suffering.

Allen Myers defines confession this way, "A declaration associated with *worship*; it may be either the *admission* of sin or the *profession* of faith."[29] I find this definition compelling for a few reasons. One, it does not limit confession to just admission of failure. Two, it connects *hope* to the regular practice of confession. Finally, I am forced to consider that true praise of God is not a monolithic expression of positive emotions. True praise of God is rich, textured, gut-wrenchingly raw, exuberantly high and lifted up, yet accessible and very much the stuff of everyday life. So, *truth to life, which aspect of confession might you need to practice in your current moment? Is there a sinful response to your trials that perhaps the Spirit of God is gently pointing out as you read this? Or do you need to confess, in faith-filled defiance, "_____ (name your trial)? You do not have the final word, Jesus does."*

What Is the Answer

The sun is chased to the far horizon by clouds of an orange and purple hue. A gentle desert breeze brushes across Job's face, drying his tears. He has lost so much. The day is now far spent and, for that matter, would be forgettable if not for the conversation occurring between Job and His God. His legs are weak as he stands to his feet and tries to process all that has just unfolded. "Did God really just answer me out of *the storm*? How ironic, powerful and humbling."

Beginning with the baseline statement, "Who is this that darkens counsel by words without knowledge? ... "Shall a faultfinder contend with the Almighty? He who argues with God, let him answer it" (Job 38:2 & 40:2, ESV). God levels the playing field and challenges Job. For all the emotional wandering and feeble expression, all the suffering of mistreatment through the words of friends and spouse, and just the sheer magnitude of loss, Job is not given an answer as to why. Does that concern you? He was bothered by it and spoke up from the beginning of the book until Job 38, where God speaks. *Friends, when God speaks, listen!* By the time we hear Job utter a brief response to God's commanding display of wisdom (Job 38–39 & 40:6–41:34), it sounds like he gets the picture; God is God and I am not, and that's a good thing. His replies (Job 40:3–5 & 42:1–6) are a picture of faith, "I had heard of you with the hearing of the ear, but now my eye sees you; therefore I despise myself, and repent in dust and ashes" (Job 42:5–6, ESV). Have you ever been there? This is something we typically see better in others than in ourselves. "They need to surrender control and let God..." or "Don't they realize that God cares even for the sparrow so why are they worried that finances are not going to pan out in this season?"

As the sun sets on the day Job's mind probes the realities and depths of his suffering. His feet are up, his belly full, and a goblet of wine is in his hand. The scene is tranquil, nothing close to what it had been in the recent past. He muses to himself, "God finally spoke. He had been silent all along. Yet in a moment of power and awesome authority, He spoke *to me*." Jemimah, Keziah, and Keren-happuch, the most beautiful new daughters God had granted Job and his wife, play wistfully on the plains behind their home. The instinct to secure their good standing with God via sacrifice now waning; Job instead sees them and thanks God, "You may have been silent, but you were most certainly not absent. You know what you're doing, and you love me. Your presence proves it."

Chapter 6—It's My World

> "Sin causes me to narrow my concern
> to the confines of my wants, my needs,
> my feelings."
>
> Paul Tripp

The late afternoon was beginning to cool, with the sun's warmth and light slowly fading into the horizon while the hustle and bustle of daily life were also drawing to a close. Most men were gone at this time of year because the various monarchies were at war defending and advancing their kingdoms with the favorable weather of the Middle East in springtime. The army of Israel had a formidable, equitable, and good king, David. The people thought highly of him because he often put their welfare and that of the kingdom ahead of his own. Time and time again they had seen him mourn the loss of soldiers and friends, inquire of the Lord as to his next battle strategy, worship God with reckless abandon, and show honor to the social outcasts (see 2 Samuel 1–10). For these reasons and more, it is a challenge to accept what transpires as a result of the beloved king's actions.

David had decided to send his capable army out to do the work he normally would participate in. *No big deal,* he thought, *I need to take some time off. I deserve it.* In the silence and tranquility of the moment, he decides to take a stroll on the roof of the palace overlooking the city. It's here that his eyes come across a woman bathing. The details of the story do not permit us to assume David was *looking* to find Bathsheba, the bathing woman, in her present state of undress. In this way the writer of Genesis had it right when he said, "…sin is crouching at your door, eager to control you. But you must subdue it and be its master" (Genesis 4:7, NLT).[30] One never needs to look for sin, for it comes like a laser-guided missile to find you. Two examples may be helpful: Men, consider going to the beach for a day of relaxation only to discover a number of women in, shall we say, culturally appropriate but not abundantly modest swimwear, setting up camp next to you. Or ladies, you are catching up on your messages at night and clearing your email inbox when you see a message advertising a steep discount on that outfit you've been eying for months. All of the sudden, in both cases, the human heart turns on itself and immediately begins to think of all the reasons why it's okay to *"just take a quick look."* This was the state of mind David inhabited on that fateful night walking the roof of his palace.

The Look

(See 2 Samuel 11–12 for the full story, I am paraphrasing here.)

Bathsheba's husband, Uriah, was off to war as a soldier in David's army under the command of Joab at the time of the incident. They had laid waste to the Ammonites and taken siege of Rabbah, their capital city. By all accounts, it was a successful endeavor. However, one that the king would miss entirely because of what was occurring back in Jerusalem. Meanwhile, on the roof of his palace, David sees Bathsheba bathing, and she is beautiful; the late afternoon sun glistening off her bare shoulders catches his eye. The crouching lion waiting at the door to David's heart is now in full attack confronting him with a life-changing decision, "Do I take a second look?" he playfully considers. I say "playfully" because that is what sin seems like at times, a playful choice that will harm no one and provide us, as its benefactor, pleasure we seem to be lacking in the moment.

Without missing a beat, David sends some servants to find out who she is. One returns with the news that she is the wife of Uriah, one of his very own soldiers. In a move characteristic of the political malaise many modern readers are accustomed to these days, he simply summons her to be brought to him and proceeds to commit adultery with her. Not long after, pregnancy is discovered and David is made aware. He goes into full-on panic, cover-my-tail mode as a result of the news. Imagine what is going through his mind: *How in the world did I end up here, getting one of my own soldier's wives pregnant? I'm the king, what was I thinking? This situation has to go away right now.* And so begins sin as a form of voluntary suffering, the results of which he must now manage.

How Is Sin Suffering

The summer after my freshman year in high school, I was to work for my dad's electrical company. It was an honor and privilege. My hopes were high for contributing to the business and making a little extra scratch that a budding young teen needs for all his hobbies. Let's be real, I wasn't the coolest kid and was simply on the lookout for a way to earn some cash. In a moment of self-effacing vulnerability let me just say that pride has been a lifelong struggle for me and will be put on full display here in a moment. From this angle, I am not afraid to tell on myself, as it were.

Dad began his weeks gathering all the guys together for a brief team meeting on Monday mornings where we'd go over the list of jobs, who was on which one, and close it all with a brief devotional or time of prayer. My father was a man who led with his heart in life and business, often treating his business like that of the church, but that is a story for another book. He was also a man who would let you learn even if it cost him and you in the process.

I recall we were wiring a new house, and I was put in the bedroom to hang a ceiling fan. I was told to shut off the power at the panel in the basement because that would ensure no additional electrical current in the junction box where I would be working. Brazen, self-assured, and cocky as the day is long, I climbed my ladder and began making the necessary wiring connections. My dad poked his head in and said, *"Son, did you shut the power off in the basement?"* I replied with utter certainty, *"I got it, Dad,"* because I assumed shutting off the switch on the wall had me covered, despite his kind warning. I pulled out my pliers and cut the wire needed to make the proper connection, and there was a huge spark that sent me reeling backward. I landed on my back from six feet up with a hole in my pliers, not to mention my pride, and Dad at the entrance saying, *"So, you never shut it off, did you?"* Still wanting to save face, I quickly replied, *"Well, I thought that the hot (the wire always containing current) was in the switch box."* I will never forget his little chuckle. It wasn't demeaning, it was *knowing*.

In the teachable moment, was my father being mean-spirited or unloving? No, he was not. Good fathers know that consequences for choices must be enacted, or children will scarcely learn what is needed to thrive in life. The same holds true for our Father God. There are consequences for sin for a few reasons. It must be stated that God honors human agency and, in order to do so, he must provide a sowing and reaping principle to our choices; this would be reason number one. He would be a manipulative God if He were to control us to avoid all sin and only chose His ways. Secondly, sin is a voluntary form of suffering simply because God said so. Scripture is replete with examples of God's kind warning, as a Father, to His stubborn and pride-filled children: "If you do _____, then _____ will happen." Consider Adam and Eve, warned not to eat of just one tree (Genesis 3), which they end up eating from, and the rest is history. If you think perfect circumstances would keep you from sin, think again; they are proof that given all advantages we still won't heed warnings! Ponder Solomon, who was warned not to worship other gods but did anyway (1 Kings 11:9–13), and discovered that all but one tribe of the kingdom would be taken, not from him, but from his son! The Apostle Paul then makes clear in Galatians 6:7 that "…God is not mocked, for whatever one sows, that will he also reap" (Galatians 6:7, ESV).

I have heard it said, "choose to sin, choose to suffer," and I agree. If I were to guess, I would say that the Apostle Peter played a role in coining that phrase. In 1 Peter 4:13–16 (ESV) he says the following:

> But rejoice insofar as you share in Christ's sufferings, that you may also rejoice and be glad when his glory is revealed. If you are insulted for the name of Christ, you are blessed, because the Spirit of glory and of God rests upon you. *But let none of you suffer as a murderer or a thief or an evildoer or as a meddler.* Yet if anyone suffers as a Christian, let him not be ashamed, but let him glorify God in that name.
>
> 1 Peter 4:13–16 (ESV)

The subject matter of our next chapter will look more closely at the suffering my faith brings and in that regard, Peter's words here will be instructive. I desire, however, to stress that here Peter is equating sin as a voluntary form of suffering; for who murders, steals, does evil, or meddles without a conscious choice? Consequences and choices aside, motive must be addressed because the question looms in our minds, "Why in the world does anyone sin if they know the potential consequences?"

Why Do We Do It?

Volumes have been written on this very topic and it is of tremendous interest to the individual who desires to walk in the freedom and fullness of all that Jesus died to give. We must agree on a baseline for the playing field to be level; otherwise, anyone could grab a reason out of thin air and build their lives around a falsehood. Foremost in this discussion is God's truth as revealed in the Bible recorded for us to have as an anchor for all time. In Psalm 51:5 (ESV), David himself declares, "Behold, I was brought forth in iniquity, and in sin did my mother conceive me" (Psalm 51:5, ESV).

You and I sin, knowing that there are consequences because it is in our nature to do so; our very DNA. Have you ever wondered why DNA is such a useful tool in the forensic analysis of a crime? The reason it is so conclusive, damning, and complete is that it cannot be altered. I can no more change my DNA than I can tell the wind to blow (or the Bears to win a Superbowl). It's locked in, part of what it means to be human.

If sin is in our DNA then how does it work itself out in the particulars? This is where identity and motives come into play and have more to say regarding our choices. The essence of sin, as the great Reformer Martin Luther once said, is believing *"...the lie of the serpent that we cannot trust the love and grace of Christ and must take matters into our own hands."* For Luther, this was all built around the idea of taking the Ten Commandments found in Exodus 20 and realizing that breaking numbers two through ten requires you to break the first, "You shall have no other God's before me."

Left to our own devices, you and I will build an identity from a gift God gives rather than from God Himself, thus having a god of our own choosing. Timothy Keller once quipped,

> The human heart is an idol factory that takes good things like a successful career, love, material possessions, even family, and turns them into ultimate things. Our hearts deify them as the center of our lives, because, we think, they can give us significance and security, safety, and fulfillment, if we attain them.[31]

Now we are getting somewhere. This resembles more closely something we'd consider enduring consequences for in order to have. Notice, according to Keller, we have now inserted good things and deified (made them God-like) them because of what we think they will deliver to us. We have, as the saying goes, bought the lie hook, line, and sinker.

Ed Welch, a counselor and faculty member at CCEF (Christian Counseling and Educational Foundation), has a seminal essay on the idea of motives and their connection to identity entitled, "Motives: Why do I do the things I do?"[32] In this work, he develops a bit more of what I am fumbling through here. He says,

> *People are complex. We've been compared to icebergs (with more under the surface than above it) and onions (with multiple layers)… Our public actions tell one story; our private intentions tell another. Behind the "what we do" of our lives—our words and actions—is the "why we do it"—our motives.*

In summary, who we are (identity) is often built around what we desire (motive). The implications are far and wide.

The discomfort our sin produces because of these choices is part of the consequence we have been discussing. We feel guilty because we know, down deep, we have done something wrong, and we need to be forgiven. We experience shame and try to hide or cover our tracks in order to save face because we believe something is fundamentally awry with us. We blame someone close to us because the spotlight on our poor choice is embarrassing or burdensome. We excuse our choice because, given the same set of circumstances, anyone would do what we did and possibly worse. We indulge because the whole scene is just hopeless; who wants an objective moral/spiritual authority when we can do just fine managing our own lives? Right? I mean, who really needs to know I can't control my desire for another drink or to click on that image after everyone has gone to bed in the home or to type out that sentence on my social media platform of choice obliterating someone for their view, which opposes mine politically?

I am aware this is not what we would like to hear. However, I urge you to calmly and reflectively sit with this difficult truth for a moment: *"What do I want and who have I hurt in the process of getting it (myself included)?"* This is the most glaring collateral of sin, relationships. The marriage gone sour, the parent who can't even speak to the child, the co-worker you'd rather avoid at the coffee break, the cousin no one talks to at family reunions, the stillness of silence and the anxiety it produces because you can't stand to be alone with your thoughts. The sheer magnitude of our sin means we cannot bear it; our shoulders lack the breadth, our will lacks the strength, our eyes lack the sight, and most poignantly—our hearts are wicked and need to be made new (Jeremiah 17:9).

Remember David. When we began this chapter, we saw a man beloved by his subjects only to learn that it all went to his head, and he made decisions that drastically affected his family for generations. Sin blinds ("In their case the god of this world has blinded the minds of the unbelievers, to keep them from seeing the light of the gospel of the glory of Christ, who is the image of God" (2 Corinthians 4:4)), hardens ("Take care, brothers, lest there be in any of you an evil, unbelieving heart, leading you to fall away from the living God. But exhort one another every day, as long as it is called "today," that none of you may be hardened by the deceitfulness of sin" (Hebrews 3:12–13)), and fools us ("The fool says in his heart, 'There is no God.' They are corrupt, they do abominable deeds; there is none who does good" (Psalm 14:1)) into presumed innocence. David was blind, not seeing the future ramifications of his sin. He was hardened to point that he took matters into his own hands and attempted to cover his tracks; ending with the murder of Uriah, Bathsheba's husband. He was a fool, mistaking the simple allegory demonstrating his sin from the prophet Nathan, who instead felt rage for the very thing he had done (see 2 Samuel 12).

What Is to Be Done?

So far what's been shared overwhelmingly points to a problem that we cannot seem to find a remedy in and of ourselves. What is it? What makes for change that would affect motive, identity, and human desire? How are we to experience the presence of God positively despite the growing evidence against us that we deserve wrath and judgment instead? The operation most necessary at this juncture is a heart transplant. In spiritual terms, straight from the pages of the Bible, "...you must be born again" (John 3:7, ESV).

The aim of this book has been to uncover how God's presence presides over our pain. More specifically for this chapter, the pain my sin has created. The assumption from the beginning has been that the reader of this work is already in a relationship with God through Christ (Ephesians 2:8–10), but finds themselves struggling to cope with their particular pain. To that end what I offer here will not be an exhaustive treatment but a primer of sorts before moving on to Christ, community, and confession; the threefold way we've been exploring that God uses to demonstrate His presence to us in our pain.

It is critical we understand our deep need, lest we drift into self-salvation and with it self-righteousness the likes for which Christ reserved his harshest critiques (see Matthew 23 for a taste of his *distaste* for spiritual pride). How do we know our need? We turn to the pages of the Bible: the Apostle Paul himself gets caught up in describing the despicable and wretched man that he is and blurts out, "who will deliver me from this body of death? Thanks be to God through Jesus Christ our Lord!" (Romans 7:24–25, ESV) We, along with Paul, are wretched and in need of saving. Returning to Luther who succinctly and powerfully states the case: *"Either sin is with you, lying on your shoulders, or it is lying on Christ, the Lamb of God. Now if it is lying on your back, you are lost; but if it is resting on Christ, you are free, and you will be saved. Now choose what you want."*

The heart is our issue. The term "heart" appears around one thousand times in the Bible. The writer of Proverbs says that it is the "wellspring of life" (Proverbs 4:23, ESV), meaning it is the center of our motives. Jesus, in the gospels of Matthew and Luke, tells us that it's like a tree that produces either good or bad fruit based on its root (see Matthew 7:15–20 and Luke 6:43–45). Later on, in Matthew, Jesus even goes so far as to say what we treasure in our hearts makes its way off our lips (Matthew 12:33–37). I guess that eliminates the "I didn't mean it" excuse when we try to apologize to someone for a careless word we spoke. In fact, we did mean it. We meant it so much that it was a treasure in our hearts, and it got coughed up in a moment of heated exchange.

Ultimately sin comes from our hearts. Jesus states it very clearly:

> And he said, "What comes out of a person is what defiles him. *For from within, out of the heart of man*, come evil thoughts, sexual immorality, theft, murder, adultery, coveting, wickedness, deceit, sensuality, envy, slander, pride, foolishness. *All these evil things come from within*, and they defile a person.
>
> Mark 7:20-22 (ESV, italics mine)

So, all of us alike are under this terrible weight, we have all sinned (Romans 3:23) and deserve the payment for those sins (Romans 6:23). However, we all can be made right with God by His grace which is a gift. Jesus took our sin on His shoulders and endured the punishment intended for us and simply asks us to receive this by faith (Romans 3:24–25) and apprentice ourselves to Jesus. He did, after all, tell His first disciples to "follow Him." There are a host of passages from the pages of scripture I could commend you to, but here are a few of my favorites: Ezekiel 36:25–28:

> I will sprinkle clean water on you, and you shall be clean from all your uncleannesses, and from all your idols I will cleanse you. And I will give you a new heart, and a new spirit I will put within you. And I will remove the heart of stone from your flesh and give you a heart of flesh. And I will put my Spirit within you, and cause you to walk in my statutes and be careful to obey my rules. You shall dwell in the land that I gave to your fathers, and you shall be my people, and I will be your God.
>
> Ezekiel 36:25–28 (ESV)

For by grace you have been saved through faith. And this is not your own doing; it is the gift of God, not a result of works, so that no one may boast. For we are his workmanship, created in Christ Jesus for good works, which God prepared beforehand, that we should walk in them.

Ephesians 2:8–10 (ESV)

But now the righteousness of God has been manifested apart from the law, although the Law and the Prophets bear witness to it— the righteousness of God through faith in Jesus Christ for all who believe. For there is no distinction: for all have sinned and fall short of the glory of God, and are justified by his grace as a gift, through the redemption that is in Christ Jesus, whom God put forward as a propitiation by his blood, to be received by faith. This was to show God's righteousness, because in his divine forbearance he had passed over former sins. It was to show his righteousness at the present time, so that he might be just and the justifier of the one who has faith in Jesus.

Romans 3:21–26

But when the goodness and loving kindness of God our Savior appeared, he saved us, not because of works done by us in righteousness, but according to his own mercy, by the washing of regeneration and renewal of the Holy Spirit, whom he poured out on us richly

through Jesus Christ our Savior, so that being
justified by his grace we might become heirs
according to the hope of eternal life

Titus 3:4–7

Study them, ruminate in the depth of God's wondrous grace to us in Christ, and let it wash over you. There will be no disappointment if you carefully and intentionally read and meditate on those passages.

His Presence in My Sin

If you may be thinking small thoughts about the heart of God for you, I'd like to gently issue an appeal. The natural bent of our humanity is seen in how we *receive love*. Consider the following scenarios: a woman is ill, and a friend makes soup for her for a week. Delivering the homemade goodness in a basket filled with scribbled notes of "get well" from her preschool children. The woman recovers and returns the basket with a thank you note, a jar of soup, and cash to cover expenses the friend incurred in caring for her. Or ponder the single mom whose vehicle is in need of repair, but the cost is too great. Some concerned loved ones pull together the funds necessary and get the needed repairs so she can safely transport her family. Weeks later, the mom, having done some sleuthing, discovered who all contributed and gives to each a gift card for a local restaurant.

We read those accounts, and perhaps we see nothing amiss. While others reading this are of the mind that those people who repaid the altruistic efforts of the generous are in fact, robbing them of the blessing to give. I wish these scenarios weren't common. Though they are fictitious, they certainly are plausible. *Truth to life, when someone does something (even something small) do you profusely thank them, try to repay them in some way, or simply receive the love they have offered? Secondly, have you ever asked, "What is it in me that feels the need to repay?"*

The truth of the matter is that we often approach God with something in hand when it comes to our sin. We just don't feel right coming to Him without having anything to offer. We think that His heart toward us is soured over our sinful choices to the degree that he disdains our return. As though His heavenly eyes roll and the disappointment of saving us is written all over His face, while He reluctantly gestures for us to come near. Is this you? I know at times it is me. It may be *true* that we feel far from him and wish we had something to offer that may placate, but the *truest* thing is that His heart is inclined toward us in our sin (1 John 2:1–2). Christ's arms are open, and His desire for me is even greater than my condemning heart is in the opposite direction. Do you believe this?

Christ and Confession

We have been tackling how the presence of God is the answer to our pain. In the case of sin, what we are calling the "voluntary form of suffering," we have seen that it is in our very DNA to do sin. We "do" sin because we want something. Relief, peace, pleasure, you name it. As a result of our choices, we make relationships with God and with others strained. So while we consider Christ, community, and confession as the means by which God communicates His presence to us in this form of suffering, I am going to lump Christ and confession together and close the chapter with the community. We experience the presence of God in our sin through repentance and surrender, being made possible by Christ's advocacy for us and our confession. Let me explain in a non-technical way how we see this working itself out from the pages of the Bible.

About fifty years after Christ's resurrection a wonderfully instructive triad of letters was penned to various congregations all across Asia Minor (present-day Turkey) by one of His own disciples, the

Apostle John. He is aged at this point, and his writing bears witness that he has some wise things to contribute. His words carefully speak to the recipient's struggle to walk out the faith they've inherited. Congregations and individuals struggling with sin are clearly in view. Who is Christ relative to the struggle with sin, and what is the role of confession in addressing it?

John writes in 1 John 2:1–2 (ESV),

My little children, I am writing these things to you so that you may not sin. But if anyone does sin, we have an advocate with the Father, Jesus Christ the righteous. He is the propitiation for our sins, and not for ours only but also for the sins of the whole world.

Like a father, John reminds the readers that when sin is chosen, the heart of Christ is for the sinner, provided they are indeed confessing Christians. For Jesus Christ the righteous to be our advocate we must call on Him in faith. Still, most of us reading this will not resonate with the terms "advocate" or "propitiation," so let me explain.

An advocate is "a person who acts as a spokesperson or representative of someone else's policy, purpose, or cause, especially before a judge in a court of law."[33] Propitiation means "...appeasing wrath and gaining the goodwill of an offended person; especially with respect to sacrifices for appeasing..."[34] We learn from Romans 6:23 that the wages or payment for our sin is death and from John 3:36 that God's wrath remains on the unrepentant person unwilling to turn to Jesus.

Let us take a step back so as not to get caught in the weeds. I think it's best to picture it like this: I am the defendant in a courtroom situation. The evidence stacked against me is overwhelming, damning really. I've committed the crime and the judge is about to throw the book at me, justifiably. What will the result be? I look on in horrified anticipation considering the fate awaiting me. Admittedly this is a very simplified sketch. However, it captures the essence of every human's situation before God. An advocate, therefore, is needed because I have the wrath of the judge and his sentence bearing down on me. Yet such a one would only be useful in the case of confessed need *because it is possible for someone to refuse advocacy.*

A few verses earlier John addressed the concern of our confession. The link between confession and the work of Christ is found right in 1 John 1:8–2:2. We can only receive cleansing from our sin, which is sorely needed when we confess its residence in us. "If we confess our sins, he is faithful and just to forgive us our sins and to cleanse us from all unrighteousness" (1 John 1:9, ESV). Furthermore, Christ can only be our advocate *if we admit our need for representation* before the Father whose wrath our sinful choice has incurred. Finally, with confession of our sin/need for saving, comes advocacy of our case before God and propitiation of his wrath over our sin.

The heart posture possessed by someone who realizes these vital truths is one of repentance and surrender. Without overstating my case, it is not the removal of sin right now that I need when suffering in this way, but the presence of God through repentance and surrender to His good design for my life. The removal of sin and suffering is a promise of God when He makes all things new (see Revelation 21), and that is a glorious day to look forward to. However, in repentance and surrender, I daily turn from self to God and say, "I want your way, your plan, your purpose for my life in this situation. Forgive me for choosing to suffer by following my own wisdom instead of yours and seeking to find fulfillment in what can never satisfy. I surrender afresh to all you have for me this day." In doing so, I am reminded of his advocacy on my behalf, trusting fully that God's wrath does not rest on me.

Truth to life, is there a sin I am actively choosing from which I need to turn to God in repentance and confess my need for the saving and cleansing work of Jesus? Take time to reflect on "knee-jerk" reactions, repetitive conflicts with loved ones, areas of known disobedience to the revealed will of God in Scripture, or those spaces of shame that plague your conscience. It is important to engage in these struggles because they reveal darkness where God wants His presence to illuminate graciously (1 John 1:5–10):

> **This is the message we have heard from him and proclaim to you, that God is light, and in him is no darkness at all. If we say we have fellowship with him while we walk in darkness, we lie and do not practice the truth. But if we walk in the light, as he is in the light, we have fellowship with one another, and the blood of Jesus his Son cleanses us from all sin. If we say we have no sin, we deceive ourselves, and the truth is not in us. If we confess our sins, he is faithful and just to forgive us our sins and to cleanse us from all unrighteousness. If we say we have not sinned, we make him a liar, and his word is not in us.**

Confess your need and abject failure in managing your life and circumstances in a way that brings glory to God. Repent or turn from those choices and seek out what God's plan or purpose in those particular situations may be by diving into the Bible and ask His Spirit to reveal what's needed. Finally, for the presence of

God to manifest in your life over sin committed, we must be a part of a community, a church. A church is simply a gathering of others who call Christ their Lord and are living life in vulnerability and with the intention of making disciples (see Matthew 28:18–20). How does the community of the redeemed help communicate the presence of God in our sin? We turn to that now.

Community

I believe one of the reasons we have such a difficult time perceiving the presence of God in our sin lies in the realization that our transactional and egocentric consumption of the Christian message drastically alters what Jesus actually intended when he came to give life abundantly (see John 10:10). Mistakenly we assume that each reference where Jesus says "you" in the Bible points to the individual instead of the corporate. Combined with the understanding of Christian discipleship as mastery of certain doctrines or biblical data, we circle the drain of our particular struggles. Never really getting the freedom or deliverance we so long for, and all the while doing it alone. There simply must be a better approach than the one many well-meaning Christians are living.

M. Robert Mulholland Jr. in his flagship work on spiritual formation says it very well:

> Scripture reveals that human wholeness is always actualized in nurturing one another toward wholeness, whether within the covenant community of God's people or in the role of God's people in healing brokenness and injustice in the world. Spiritual formation "for the sake of others" will be seen to move against the grain of a *privatized* and *individualized* religion and

the deep seeded belief that spiritual life is a matter between the individual and God. There can be no wholeness in the image of Christ *which is not incarnate in our relationships with others*, both in the body of Christ and in the world.[35]

There are many ways God uses the community of believers for the formation of Christ's image in us, and I will seek to address a few of the prominent ones. However, we must dispense with the notion that my growth in grace is a private affair. We pursue the rest he offers *together* so that, in an ultimate sense, we are accountable to him. Hebrews 4:11–13 says it this way:

So let us do our best to enter that rest. But if we disobey God, as the people of Israel did, we will fall. For the word of God is living and powerful. It is sharper than the sharpest two-edged sword, cutting between soul and spirit, between joint and marrow. It exposes our innermost thoughts and desires. Nothing in all creation is hidden from God. Everything is naked and exposed before his eyes, and he is the one to whom we are accountable.

Hebrews 4:11–13 (NLT)[36]

The following are some of the ways God works through others to convey his presence to us in our sins. We will look at how Jesus exemplified all of them and see what it means for us.

First of all, commitment over the long haul has always been a vital component for ongoing relational depth. In his life, Jesus prayerfully selected twelve disciples with whom he would share his life (see Luke

6:12–16). Upon selection, they set out on an uncertain, perilous, and unprecedented journey. As time progressed, Jesus repetitively modeled for them what it was like to be committed, compassionate, and for the good of others. Often his disciples would argue over inane things (see Luke 22:24–30), have their mothers request odd things (Matthew 20:20–28), make promises they couldn't keep (Matthew 26:35), and then break those promises (Matthew 26:69–75). For his part, Jesus remained steadfastly committed even when sinned against. This reveals what I believe is of utmost importance for us to experience the presence of God in our sin; we can't just be taught about commitment, we must learn it along the way.

You and I begin to grasp a little more clearly, the love of God for us and His presence in our lives because others are committed to us long-term. The reality we have all experienced at one time or another is a relationship that lacked any real perseverance through strife, disagreement, or wounding, all of which our sin has caused between God and ourselves. A quick perusal of the four Gospel accounts reveals Jesus' choice to "stay in love" (a phrase my wife's mentor used with her years ago about how to endure difficulty in a relationship) when all others would presumably give up. It stands to reason, then, His presence in our sin is communicated deeply by another believer who is not so disgusted with me but my sin. Another fellow struggler, who puts their arm on my shoulder and says, "I don't even know what to say right now except thank you. Thank you for sharing about that deep dark struggle. Would you mind if I prayed with you right now to simply receive the forgiveness and cleansing available from God?"

Is this not what we long for in a relationship? A shame-shattering friend who acknowledges the grim nature of our sin-dominated reality but echoes the fact of Jesus' own blood speaking a better word of forgiveness and cleansing. These are not textbook scraps gleaned from a PowerPoint presentation by a professor who only has a connection with my mind. These are experiences of God's grace in Christ through the community of the redeemed. Finally, freedom from that sin that has so entangled you and me is coming into view, and, in part, it is because of others.

Secondly, Christians are uniquely gifted (see Romans 12; 1 Corinthians 12, 14; and Ephesians 4) to make up a body, and a body cares for its own. When someone is committed over the long haul to us, they gain our trust, and with it, our vulnerable expressions of need when we are wrecked by our sin. These deep friends ask us hard questions about the way our actions are communicating louder than our words. Love-governed Christians are sacrificial and available to help, willing to tell us the hard truth in a gentle way. Holy Spirit-led Christians are prayerful and supportive, they realize the importance of bringing us before the throne of grace where we can get the help we need. *Truth to life, are you this kind of friend in Christ to at least a few other Christians?* The best way to begin seeing this as a reality in your own life is to do so for others. Here is a quick checklist of what that may look like in your life: Make a relational commitment to check on another believing friend in sin. Two, offer your own struggles in mutuality. Third, with the help of God's spirit, meet together frequently. Finally, hold their stories and struggles well by not sharing details with others.

When Jesus ascended to His Father the author of Acts tells us that He informed the disciples of how His Holy Spirit was now going to inhabit them; making them a powerful band of witnesses for His sake. Not long after Peter and John, a few of His disciples, are doing the very thing Jesus said they would by bearing witness about Him. As a result, they are questioned, beaten, and released. This is where we are headed next. How could these fearful and failing men emerge from the shadows and rejoice when persecuted? It seems backward, doesn't it?

CHAPTER 7—LIVING FOR ANOTHER WORLD

"Jesus Christ did not suffer so that you would not suffer. He suffered so that when you suffer, you'll become more like Him."

Timothy Keller

The dusty streets of Jerusalem were busy with the normal daily activities. Business was being conducted, civil servants were doing their duty, children were playing in the alleyways, Pentecost had just finished, and the scads of foreigners in town for the festival were still milling about. There was nothing observers from the outside would catch at a glance. "Ordinary" would describe the situation. Ordinary with one minor catch.

There were rumblings, conversations among a growing number of people concerning Jesus Christ of Nazareth. In the not-too-distant past, there had been a great commotion over Him being crucified with some other criminals. Was it justly done? He seemed like an innocent man. More recently His followers had been filled with a strange fire that caused some to speak in languages they clearly did not know, allowing many visitors to hear about God's mighty works in their *native* language. This guy Peter, an Apostle of Jesus, gets up, explains the phenomena, and the little group of about one hundred twenty explodes to around three thousand! Everyone seems to be on board, listening to teaching, spending time together eating and praying, and meeting with one another in homes. The mighty works they had heard about were now happening in front of their very eyes, and not one of them was in need.

The catch was the fact Jesus had been crucified for saying and doing the very same things these followers of His were now doing. Surely this was going to reach a tipping point, and the Pharisees, Sadducees, elders, and scribes (the political-religious ruling establishment of the day) were bound to do something. How long could they stay silent about the man and His followers who they *already* tried to kill in order to quell? The situation was fraught with tension, and it seemed only a small spark could ignite the kindling that any conscientious observer sensed was all around. Enter Apostle Peter.

In short order and avoiding all niceties, Peter goes toe to toe with the establishment and says, "and you killed the Author of life, whom God raised from the dead. To this we are witnesses" (Acts 3:15, ESV).[37] Dale Carnegie, author of the now-famous *How to Win Friends and Influence People*, would certainly have needed a special seminar or two alone with Peter to let him know that this is not the best route to take if you want to get people in your corner for a cause. In fact, this will likely get you killed, considering the present hostile climate in which he was. However, Peter cannot help but speak about what he has seen and heard (Acts 4:20). Escalating quickly in the very next scene, we see Peter and John detained and questioned before the council of leaders.

This story of Peter and John unfolds over a few chapters, and I encourage you to pick up your own Bible and read it, perhaps before continuing here, because it lays a foundation. Peter, who only a few months earlier had denied Jesus three times at the threat of being associated with Him is now front and center of the movement that will eventually be the cause of His own death. How does this happen in one's life? What are the simple observations we can make from the text that will aid us if/when we come to our own hour of need where we are facing opposition and mistreatment for our faith in Jesus?

What Do We See?

The opening lines of Acts chapter four say, "And as they were speaking to the people, the priests and the captain of the temple and the Sadducees came upon them, greatly annoyed because they were teaching the people and proclaiming in Jesus the resurrection from the dead" (Acts 4:1–2, ESV).[38] As a matter of first importance their proclamation was "in Jesus." *No other name will invoke such polar reactions as Jesus.* Peter clearly states why only a few verses later by saying, "...there is no other name under heaven given among men by which we must be saved" (Acts 4:12, ESV).[39] So the first observation we can make regarding persecution is simply that fidelity to the person and work of Jesus Christ is irksome and will incur mistreatment no matter what.

The narrative progresses, and an unexpected response from the antagonists catches us off guard. "Now when they saw the boldness of Peter and John and perceived that they were uneducated, common men, they were astonished. And they recognized that *they had been with Jesus*... they had nothing to say in opposition" (Acts 4:13–14, ESV).[40] When someone is greatly annoyed or highly offended usually reactions like this are not the result. These men, however, derived their boldness from the presence of Jesus. Is this not the very thing we are after in our pursuit in this book? How does the presence of God reign over my pain, whatever form it is? The disciples had seen this modeled; time in His presence prepares and sustains through seasons of outpouring or persecution. Jesus often withdrew to get alone with God for prayer, solitude, and comfort (Mark 1:35, Luke 5:15–16, Mark 1:45, 3:13, 8:27, and 9:2). His disciples were frequently with Him or searching to find Him. Uncommon boldness when your life is threatened can only mean hope and comfort are not tethered to the temporal.

The disciples had seen Jesus spend time with His father and witnessed how it impacted and prepared Him. Now, in the Acts narrative, we are beginning to see how they are putting this right into action. Multiple times from Jesus' own lips, we hear Him indicate He can only do and say what the Father tells Him. His disciples now follow suit while they are being cross-examined and confirm to their accusers silence is not an option. "We cannot but speak of what we have seen and heard" (Acts 4:20, ESV). Instead of dousing the fire beginning to rage, it fueled it. The believers around Peter and John grew more emboldened and began asking God for additional strength to speak with clarity and conviction. The gospel continues to spread at a rapid rate, and future run-ins with the establishment only serve to embolden them more! Indeed, one of the most impactful aspects for me of this narrative is when the apostles are arrested, beaten, and freed *yet* still rejoicing! I have to be brutally honest… to complain at the first sign of mistreatment and call it a "right" is a near art form in our day making this more than just a pedestrian struggle.

Christ

We have noted some of what the disciples had a front-row seat to, namely the way that Jesus approached His impending arrest, trial, conviction, and murder, all of which were unjust! The strength that Jesus gained came from His time away with the Father. This strength was put into practice, and to the test, once the powers that be determined He was a threat. He was slandered, openly opposed, misquoted, run out of town, and a host of other experiences all before the crucifixion was set into motion. How did Jesus Himself model perseverance for us at this moment? As we work through the example of Christ, the community of faith, and our joint confession with regard to persecution, I'd like to propose some practices we see from Jesus as our focus: prayer as time with God, discernment, boldness, and mercy. These are, by no means, exhaustive, but they will provide us with some navigational buoys, if you will.

Luke 5:16 (NIV) notes, "But Jesus often withdrew to lonely places and prayed." A recent study by the Journal of General Internal Medicine[41] had a chilling observation that is mimicked in most of our prayer lives. The researchers observed that doctors interrupted patients on average within eleven seconds of them first speaking. In fact, in 64 to 80 percent of visits, the doctor did not even ask the patient why they were there in the first place. Can you imagine a situation in which your faith in the loving, protective, secure love of God is grown by that sort of impatience?

If Jesus withdrew to lonely places to pray and is even said to have spent the entire night in prayer, how could that be accomplished if one party felt the need to interrupt within eleven seconds? To spend time in prayer requires not a laundry list of the ways that God can get on board with my agenda but a slow, methodical, and gentle laying down of mine in order to align more fully with His will. I have often heard it said, "Most of us don't hear God speak because we have already decided what he is going to say." Jesus, all-powerful, all-wise, all-gracious, and all-knowing, illustrates perfectly for us what it is to depend on God. I want you to say this out loud, "God, I depend on you" (seriously, say it with conviction and joy). Then, lean into that reality and allow God to speak as you pray. *Truth to life, am I afraid of what will be spoken in prayer as I sit silently with God? What might he ask of me I am not ready to do, give up, or go for? Finally, am I forgetful of my place and instead find myself like the doctors in the study, interrupting God every eleven seconds? What would my interruptions say about my faith, my dependence, and where it is aimed?*

Jesus also displayed incredible discernment and boldness in the face of what would otherwise be crushing. Two passages will guide our understanding as they illustrate snippets of Jesus' perseverance through trial. Isaiah 53:7 (ESV), written about seven hundred years before Christ, predicts, "He was oppressed and afflicted, yet he did not open his mouth; he was led like a lamb to the slaughter, and as a sheep before her shearers is silent, so he did not open his mouth" (Isaiah 53:7, ESV). Mark picks up the fulfillment of this powerful prophecy when he says in 14:61 (ESV), "But he remained silent and made no answer. Again the high priest asked Him, "Are you the Christ, the Son of the Blessed?" The epitome of discernment, Jesus remained silent before those who would accuse, condemn and murder Him. Discernment, in this case, illustrates to whom Jesus' was anchored. Let me explain: if Jesus had lacked discernment at that moment, He would have snapped back at the high priest and put him in his place, thus confirming His "anchor" was in His own strength and agenda. However, by remaining silent in this case, Jesus pulled back the veil for all His followers, revealing His true allegiance was to God and His plan, even if it cost Him.

How then are we to witness the boldness of Jesus if He remains silent in moments of accusation that are clearly false? Keep reading the account of Mark, for He says in the very next verse, "I am," said Jesus. "And you will see the Son of Man sitting at the right hand of the Mighty One and coming on the clouds of heaven" (NIV). Boldness, here, is quite literally Jesus not cowering in the face of intimidation or persecution, but instead aligning His internal faith with His external actions. *Truth to life, when do I get defensive or self-justifying in my speech or actions? Has there been a time I have not connected my internal faith and my external actions because I was fearful of how someone might respond?*

Finally, Jesus displayed life-altering mercy to those around Him. Often it was said when He saw oppressed people as they entered a town that he had compassion (mercy) on them because they were helpless. The example of Jesus displaying mercy most connects to what we are discussing here in the brutal and humiliating cross leading to His death. After being wrongly convicted, He is drug away and made to carry the instrument of His death to the place of His execution. Mocked mercilessly by those in power and publicly scorned while

He trod that path; Jesus doesn't say anything. However, once He is nailed to the cross, onlookers either gratified or horrified, He endures one last verbal assault from two despicable and properly convicted outlaws. The thieves sharing space with Him on their own crosses hurl insults and mockery. One of them, however, catches himself in the folly and humbly asks Jesus to remember him.

> One of the criminals who were hanged railed at him, saying, "Are you not the Christ? Save yourself and us!' But the other rebuked him, saying, 'Do you not fear God, since you are under the same sentence of condemnation? And we indeed justly, for we are receiving the due reward of our deeds; but this man has done nothing wrong." And he said, "Jesus, remember me when you come into your kingdom."
>
> Luke 23:39–42

Truth to life, when I experience mistreatment and it turns out I was right, is it more common for me to hold or release that person? Forgiveness is releasing someone from the obligation to pay.

We make people pay relationally in various ways: ignoring, talking down to, or never giving them a chance to prove they've changed, to name a few.

Community

The term "church" in the New Testament comes from the Greek word *ekklesia*, which means a gathering of called-out ones. As the community of believers here on earth, we are gathered together into smaller congregations so as to more effectively accomplish the mission of God for the particular contexts we find ourselves in. This is important because the mission is going to look much different in urban Los Angeles than in rural Indiana or in war-torn Afghanistan than in the mountain villages in the Himalayas. None is more significant in God's eyes than the other, just different. Each will have their own form of opposition or persecution to the message of Jesus; remember, we established that He alone is the most polarizing figure in all human history.

To wait together in prayer before moving is an act of faith. Acts thirteen demonstrates how the first believers in Jesus lived this out. A bunch of gifted prophets and teachers, including the Apostle Paul, were in the Antioch church worshipping and fasting. God spoke for Barnabas and Saul (Paul) to be sent out on a missionary journey. The church took up a dedicated time of fasting and prayer prior to sending them out, really they *waited* on God and acted in accord with His will and plan. I encourage you to see these as the practical outworking of faith in the real world when you read them.

> **There was tremendous opposition to the message of the Gospel in those early days, as there is now, and preparation, not reaction is the call to Christ's church in the present moment.**

We should be on high alert these days; worshipping, fasting, and praying for specific direction for God. *Truth to life, do my daily, and personal practices really allow God to interrupt and direct? What about the church you are part of? Are you regularly gathering with others to worship, wait, and seek God?* You see, one of the ways that His presence is made known through persecution is by way of invitation and acknowledgment. Acts 16 serves as a portrait for reminding us of God's invitation. Should we seek him we will find him. Paul and Silas are in prison and around midnight they are praying and worshipping the Lord. Just pause. How far outside the realm of reality is that statement for you when it comes to hardship and mistreatment? Nonetheless, there they are, just being rock-solid witnesses for Jesus. Do you know what the result was? The church at Philippi gets planted! You can read about it in Acts 16:22–40 and then the letter to the Philippians as well. So, worship God with abandon, not caring who sees or hears, it may be more evangelistic than you realize. It led to a conversion of a jailer and his family and the beginning of a church in the first century, what about the twenty-first century?

Confession

We have seen Jesus displaying a prayerful life, discernment demonstrating the object of His anchoring faith, boldness in the face of opposition and mistreatment, and mercy for those near Him. The community of faith around us begins to drive home these vital truths as we invite and acknowledge his presence among us through worship, prayer, and fasting. What role ought confession play in this final look at God's presence over the pain of persecution? Recalling how confession is not just an admittance of wrongdoing but also a *declaration of agreement*, perhaps it is best for us to return to the simple yet powerful phrase, "I depend on you." King David, who was no stranger to oppression, accusation, and enmity, penned a Psalm forever preserved for us as a confession in persecution. Psalm 7 is replete with deep faith, honest anguish, a heartfelt confession of sin, and abiding trust. Ultimately, it is David saying, "I depend on you."

> I come to you for protection, O LORD my
> God. Save me from my persecutors—rescue
> me! If you don't, they will maul me like a lion,
> tearing me to pieces with no one to rescue

me. O LORD my God, if I have done wrong or am guilty of injustice, if I have betrayed a friend or plundered my enemy without cause, then let my enemies capture me. Let them trample me into the ground and drag my honor in the dust. Arise, O LORD, in anger! Stand up against the fury of my enemies! Wake up, my God, and bring justice! Gather the nations before you. Rule over them from on high. The LORD judges the nations. Declare me righteous, O LORD, for I am innocent, O Most High! End the evil of those who are wicked, and defend the righteous. For you look deep within the mind and heart, O righteous God. God is my shield, saving those whose hearts are true and right. God is an honest judge. He is angry with the wicked every day. If a person does not repent, God will sharpen his sword; he will bend and string his bow. He will prepare his deadly weapons and shoot his flaming arrows. The wicked conceive evil; they are pregnant with trouble and give birth to lies. They dig a deep pit to trap others, then fall into it themselves. The trouble they make for others backfires on them. The violence they plan falls on their own heads. I will thank the LORD because he is just; I will sing praise to the name of the LORD Most High.

Psalm 7 (NLT)

The ultimate and lasting truth we must confess is the Scriptures over our lives and sufferings. David gives us a tremendous leg up with this Psalm, and we would do well to return to it, or others of them, often for comfort. *Truth to life, what words give me most comfort when I am oppressed or marginalized? Is there another believer with whom I can memorize and read God's word together?*

Confession that affirms, in an active sense, the involvement and compassion of God will prove to be of inestimable worth for those experiencing any form of persecution. However, before we move on and conclude the chapter, one thought on how persecution can feel. All forms of suffering develop mechanisms that trip up the saint of God and discourage. Persecution or marginalization of the Christian is no exception to this rule for the punishment we face for our faith may mistakenly be associated with God angrily smiting us. It is important, at this juncture, to recall the words and life of Jesus. In John 16:33, He said, "In this world, you will have trouble. But take heart! I have overcome the world" (NIV). The only Holy and perfect human to ever walk the face of the earth experienced the harshest and most comprehensive persecution so that when we suffer, we could become like Him. It was not an angry and abusive move of God the Father toward His son; rather, it was the perfection of justice and mercy coming together in order that sin would be paid for and our hope forever anchored in Him.

A Gentle Warning

Brother Yun, a Chinese Christian born in the late 1950s, came to faith in Jesus when he was a sixteen-year-old as a result of his father's illness and mother's despair. Upon salvation, his appetite for the Word of God was insatiable. However, his family did not own a Bible in Communist China. The danger was great, but his desire for the teachings of Jesus recorded for all time, the way his mom described the Bible, could not be stopped. He prayed intently for one hundred days which culminated in a vision about a Bible and two missionaries showing up at his door secretly to deliver it as a result of a vision of their own miles away leading them directly to the Yun household! Brother Yun prioritized the ingestion and memorization of God's words which led to a call in his life to share the Gospel with those around him, even at a great potential cost to himself.

For his part in promoting the Gospel, he was arrested by police regularly and was thrown into prison three times. These prison stays included: solitary confinement, being beaten with electric batons, kicked, trampled, and having needles pressed under his fingernails. He was also publicly shamed by having a cross tied to his back and being flaunted through the city. Finally, during his third imprisonment, he was beaten badly with the intent to cripple him and prevent a future escape. Still, by God's incredible grace and sustained through the ongoing presence of the Holy Spirit he was able to miraculously escape on May 5th, 1997. What he has experienced has caused some to regard him as the most persecuted believer in China.

If you have ever read *The Heavenly Man* by Brother Yun chronicling his experience in Communist China as a Christian, where I gained some of the above insights, you may wonder if he thought he was the most persecuted believer in China. Such a statement is hard to quantify and is not the aim of this book. However, Yun himself tips his hand as to the direction he leans when he says the following in the book,

> I didn't suffer for Jesus in prison. No! I was with Jesus, and I experienced His very real presence, joy, and peace every day. It's not those in prison for the sake of the gospel who suffer. The person who suffers is he who never experiences God's intimate presence.[42]

It would be fitting to close with the following thought. Do I agree with Brother Yun? In essence, he is saying, "to miss the presence of God is to suffer the greatest pain." In our instant gratification world, with two-day shipping, online grocery ordering, tap-to-pay, and much more by way of zero downtime when it comes to fulfilling desires, would we even know if we missed The Presence? This is a conversation of some importance, don't you think? Aversion to pain is one thing, stopping to even feel pain is another, while self-medicating our way out of or around pain may really be the issue. The pain of persecution for our faith is the primary observation I am making. Tailoring the way and practices of Jesus so that his claims and the resulting impact on our lives are softened or removed because they may appear offensive or intrusive is largely what has happened in western Christianity.

Brother Yun is proposing that being canceled, kicked, or killed for the sake of the Gospel is lesser in its scope and severity than missing the presence of God altogether.

Grasping this reality is what gave Jesus the foresight to persevere in his own persecution AND it developed his compassion for those around him. God's presence with us through persecution is really greater and more comprehensively joy-producing than never experiencing any form of persecution at all.

CHAPTER 8—PUTTING IT ALL TOGETHER

> "God is able to penetrate and intertwine
> Himself within the fibers of the human self in
> such a way that those who are enveloped in
> His loving companionship will never be alone."
> —Dallas Willard

We come to the end of our brief exploration concerning our pain and God's presence. Arriving at this place without having gained a deeper and more faith-filled grasp of God with us would be tragic at worst and an exercise in futility at best, spinning our wheels, so to speak. How can we, along with the Psalmist of old, say, "You make known to me the path of life; in your presence there is fullness of joy; at your right hand are pleasures forevermore" (Psalm 16:11, ESV). Fullness of joy... really? I think the clue, which begs further investigation and deep heart submission, lies in what the author reveals in the first two verses of the Psalm. He begins by saying, "Preserve me, O God, for in you I take refuge. I say to the LORD, "You are my Lord; *I have no good apart from you*" (Psalm 16:1–2, ESV). When one truly believes that God is good and their only good, then what could possibly be taken from them in suffering? Without a doubt, this is what it means for God's presence to preside over our pain.

Suffering in all its forms is insular, causing one to focus more narrowly on himself. Take the following three examples and see if you would agree with me from my own experience in counseling. Before you read, please know all examples have names and details changed to protect privacy.

The unplanned hardship. Jane holds her newborn son in her arms lovingly; she locks eyes with the helpless lad. Their bond is immediate, deep, and oh so tender. Damon grows up strong, like his mother in many ways. His innovation and creative tendencies rock the industry of the career he loves. Jane's heart swells with pride as she watches her son accomplish things that one only reads about or sees in movies. "Could this really be my son? It seems so crazy that his knowledge and personality are so overwhelmingly magnetic, and the opportunities he's being given are so staggering." She's right; his personality is perfectly suited for leadership.

In a turn, no one could predict, however, a diagnosis, which has no cure, much less a positive prognosis begins to ravage the young man's body. Before he even hits his prime, the fire of life is snuffed out. Leaving his mom to experience debilitating grief, "Why, God? I look around, and people are laughing, enjoying life, existing without this huge hole in their hearts caused by the loss of a child. No one gets me." Jane muses, "How is this going to build my faith?"

The consequences of sin are hardships. Jason is pastor of a small rural church where he has happily served for more than fifteen years. Throughout those arduous and rewarding years, because of his faithful commitment, he has had the incredible privilege of raising spiritual children. The relationship he shares with them is full of service to others, truth, and love. Side by side he has labored with the students of the ministry. Now, as those students are coming of age, finding careers, spouses, and having children of their own, the fruit of all his work is coming into view. He and his wife are providing premarital counseling for many former "youth groupers." It is humbling and beautiful in its sowing and reaping imagery.

Behind the scenes, sadly, Jason had been tending another garden, one of lust, specifically nurturing the craving of his flesh for pornographic content. In a moment of brokenness and repentance, he comes to the board of elders, who oversees his employment and confesses his sin. News of his struggle trickles its way down to the students he has loved and served for so long. For the most part, there is a favorable reaction, grace is actually put into practice, forgiveness is given and received; reconciliation occurs. Still, there remains an inner circle of some of his closest students through the years. They are hurt at what feels like a betrayal. Jason is overcome almost daily by condemning shouts of the enemy of his soul. "I've ruined the name of Jesus because of my want for pleasure and escape, what is wrong with me? Could God ever want me again? I thought repentance brought freedom?"

The persecution hardship. Ahmad came to the United States as an immigrant following a dream of education leading to a career in engineering. He is the first of his family to depart Syria. The move caused immediate friction between his father and him. It has been six years since he first set foot on American soil, and Ahmad has been busy building a new life for himself as his own family became increasingly distant from him and caustic with their cutting remarks. He used to brush it off, saying there is a cultural and language divide that is not easily overcome. However, more recently his father discovered that he has been going to an evangelical church that preaches about Jesus being the way, truth, and life. This will not stand. In direct contradiction to the Islamic faith, their family has adhered to for generations, is Ahmad's newfound faith. There will be a reckoning. He knows it.

Faced with an unsettling reality, Ahmad must choose whether he will bend to his father's wishes, removing all Bibles and any reference to Jesus from his home when they come to visit next month. He labors over the prospect that he may have to tell his dad, "No, I am sorry, I will not remove my convictions in order to accommodate for your comfort." Finally, he makes up his mind to hold the line and expresses to his parents, lovingly, "You are welcome to stay, but I respectfully decline to take references to Jesus or my Bibles out of my home. If you would like to talk further about that, I'd be happy to." The response he receives in reply from his father cuts incredibly deep. "I do not think I can call you our son any longer. Your allegiance to the Christian faith will render our further relationship impossible." Ahmad is broken. Crushed in spirit and increasingly finds himself questioning the very faith which pushed his parents to the breaking point of their association with him. Who will truly be there for him now? How will he persevere?

What Now?

First, it must be noted upon reading these short stories that suffering in any form has the potential to turn us in on ourselves. Briefly recall where each of the characters was left at the conclusion of their short story. Jane thinks no one gets her grief and in turn, is questioning the very faith she professes. Jason's shame is crushing and he has a real bout with condemnation even after he has demonstrated repentance. Ahmad is riding along the ridge of depression and perhaps fear as he contemplates further ramifications of persevering faith. Each one is not thinking wrongly, they are just a smidge more interested in themselves. The interest is driven by how no one understands them or how they may not even want to be understood. Suffering is truly isolating. This very statement, suffering is truly isolating, is far deeper than any of us can grasp. It gets to the heart of what the enemy of our souls seeks to do with our suffering, namely, "God doesn't care about you or your plight. See, he's got his back turned in silence." For a brief treatment of this, I encourage you to look toward the Psalms. Forty-two is so poignant as the author cries out concerning his tears being the bearer of bad news, "Where is your God?" Isolated. Alone. Left to fend for ourselves. Suffering is isolating.

In addition to the isolation of suffering, we combine the reality of how the three forms often intermingle. I do not think it is outside the realm of plausible for any of us who profess Jesus, for example, to say that we have experienced times of trial physically while attendant to it was a temptation to escape or indulge that we almost felt in our bones. I mean simply this, misery loves company. If I am suffering from an ongoing illness that has no expiration date, I may find that indulging in pornography allows for an escape to pleasure, causing me to forget my ailment momentarily. Often we can point to how one form of suffering bled into another, which pushes to the fore our most pressing question since page one of our exploration.

The question before us now is, "What have we learned?" We know that God's presence is the answer to our particular pain, yet we are short-sited, and executive summaries are often needed to jog our way-weary memories when theory is meant to move into practice. Below is a diagram I scribbled on a piece of paper that may help jog your own memory when a form (or two) of pain comes your way.

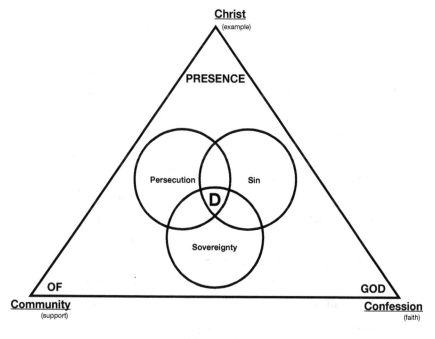

Figure 1

In our illustration, we have a very basic representation of you and me as disciples of Jesus. This can be seen with the "D" at the center of the chart. Years ago as a youth pastor at Northfield Christian Fellowship in Tremont, Illinois, I recall being in a dimly lit room on a Wednesday night. We had been unpacking the idea of following Jesus as a way of life. The church was (and is) full of amazing families who have raised their children to love God and love others. Many report making a faith commitment at an early age. This particular night I was concerned the students needed to be challenged, so I asked a simple question. "Who here would say they are Christians?" Many, if not all of the hands, shot up. I paused and then asked, "How many would say that you are disciples?" One hand... that's it, sheepishly rose. With befuddlement written across my face, I inquired what the disconnect was. One of the students blurted out, "I said Christian because Disciple just sounds so much more serious." Friends, we are disciples of Jesus. A disciple is simply defined as a learner. I am learning to love Jesus and walk as He did alongside others.

Secondly, we see how our three forms of suffering converge on us as disciples in a Venn diagram[43] illustrating the intermingling nature of hardship (persecution, sin, sovereignty). Remember, misery loves company and trouble loves the disciple. Jesus warned us of this in John 16:33 when he said that we will have trouble in this world but He is the one who overcame. We would do well to heed our Lord and not be surprised when it comes upon us (see also 1 Peter 4:12). It often serves to make us more like Jesus.

An attribute of God is His omnipresence. This basically means that He is everywhere at once and as an obvious implication, never far from us as His children. We see this in the illustration above that while we are surrounded by troubles, His presence encompasses us as His beloved children. If we have learned anything let it begin with this; He is here. Now. With me as I write and with you as you read.

So we affix our attention and cultivate our affections to appreciate and recognize the immanence of the Lord. The most precious of all truths we affirm at Christmastime is "Immanuel, God with us."

As a babe in the manger, as a friend at the table, as a man on the cross, as a victor striding joyfully out of the grave! He is with you!

Finally, the threefold means of communicating His presence[44] that God uses: Christ, community, and confession are seen at the corners of our diagram. The Apostle John reminds us in 1 John 2:6, "whoever says he abides in him ought to walk in the same way in which he walked" (1 John 2:6, ESV). In life and death, *Christ* Jesus is our supreme example. He has experienced two of the three kinds of suffering we have been exploring and is the only answer to our entanglement with sin. Jesus, in all ways, is the linchpin of our salvation, growth in grace, and the demonstrable mercy of God toward us.

The *community* of other believers we are a part of serves an important function as well. We are able to lean on them for support as we deal with sin, struggle with the inexplicable hardships we face, which God allows, and are increasingly pushed to the margins of society suffering mistreatment for what we believe. I like to say that God has His people everywhere, and He's not afraid to use them. We encounter the presence of God through His people.

Confession is the ongoing rehearsal of the goodness of God in our lives. It cultivates faith to speak in agreement with the promises of God found throughout His word. It is an act of war against the enemy of our souls who would seek to discourage us with the following types of statements or questions in our suffering: If God really loved you, He would not allow this to happen to you. If God loved you, He would know that all you really want is to be happy and would be ok with just one more drink. Why love God when it will end in pain or marginalization? *Confession*, when combined with the *example of Jesus* and the support of the *community* becomes an effective weapon!

A Father's Relentless Love

Armenia is a small nation between the Caspian and Black seas and a former Soviet republic. In 1988 there was a devastating earthquake (actually two) measuring 6.9 and 5.8 in magnitude.[45] The effects were devastating. Killing nearly 60,000 people and destroying nearly half a million buildings. The story is told[46] of a father who had dropped his son at school earlier that day. Samuel could not get ahold of anyone at the school and fearing the worst returned to what was now rubble. He knew the general location of his son Armand's classroom and began to make way to it. Once there, he began digging with his bare hands.

Samuel dug for ten hours until the evening came and largely by himself. Other parents had come with flowers and were already grieving the loss of their children. Temperatures began to plunge, making conditions even less favorable, yet it did not deter Samuel from digging. After about thirty-six hours of hard labor, with his hands bloodied, he broke into the classroom where Armand and thirteen of his classmates were. In a surprising move, Armand did not initially run to greet his father. Instead, he turned to his classmates and said, "I told you my father would always be there for me."

In the rubble of our lives caused by the suffering we face and our responses to it, our Father digs.

He relentlessly, when others have long given up hope and simply walked away, pursues us with His presence.

Endnotes

[1] John 16:33 ESV

[2] Psalm 16:11 ESV

[3] 1 John 4:18 ESV

[4] Philippians 3:8-9 ESV

[5] Romans 10:9-10 ESV

[6] Manser, Martin H., *Zondervan Dictionary of Bible Themes. The Accessible and Comprehensive Tool for Topical Studies.* Grand Rapids, MI: Zondervan, 1999.

[7] Hebrews 11:1 ESV

[8] Walvoord, John F., and Roy B. Zuck, Dallas Theological Seminary. *The Bible Knowledge Commentary: An Exposition of the Scriptures.* Wheaton, IL: Victor Books, 1985.

[9] Walls, David, and Max Anders. *I & II Peter, I, II & III John, Jude.* Vol. 11. Holman New Testament Commentary. Nashville, TN: Broadman & Holman Publishers, 1999.

[10] Oxford Dictionary of English
Copyright © 2010, 2020 by Oxford University Press. All rights reserved.

[11] Psalm 119:67 ESV

[12] 1 Peter 4:12–19 ESV

[13] Romans 15:4 ESV

[14] Deuteronomy 8:2 ESV

[15] Deuteronomy 8:14 ESV

[16] Deuteronomy 8:15-16 ESV

[17] 2 Timothy 3:12 ESV

[18] Hebrews 13:5-6 ESV

[19] Romans 8:32 NLT

[20] Matthew 27:46 ESV

[21] Isaiah 43:2 ESV

[22] Job 1:1 ESV

[23] Job 1:13-22 ESV

[24] Job 2:4 ESV

[25] Job 2:10 NLT

[26] Strong, James. *A Concise Dictionary of the Words in the Greek Testament and The Hebrew Bible*. Bellingham, WA: Logos Bible Software, 2009.

[27] *Ibid.*

[28] Card, Michael. *A Sacred Sorrow: Reaching Out to God in the Lost Language of Lament*. Colorado Springs, CO: Navpress, 2005.

[29] Myers, Allen C. *The Eerdmans Bible Dictionary*. Grand Rapids, MI: Eerdmans, 1987.

[30] Genesis 4:7 NLT

[31] Keller, Timothy J. *Counterfeit Gods: The Empty Promises of Money, Sex, and Power, and the Only Hope that Matters*. Penguin Books, 2009

[32] https://thechapelblogdotcom.files.wordpress.com/2022/04/f6853-motives-by-welch.pdf (accessed 8/29/2022)

[33] Thompson, Jeremy. *Bible Sense Lexicon: Dataset Documentation*. Bellingham, WA: Faithlife, 2015.

[34] Ibid.

[35] Mulholland Jr., Robert M. *Invitation to a Journey*. Downer's Grove, IL. Intervarsity Press, 2016.

[36] Hebrews 4:11-13 NLT

[37] Acts 3:15 ESV

[38] Acts 4:1-2 ESV

[39] Acts 4:12 ESV

[40] Acts 4:13-14 ESV

41 https://www.forbes.com/sites/brucelee/2018/07/22/ how-long-you-can-talk-before-your-doctor-interrupts- you/?sh=749e17bd1443 (accessed 8/29/2022)

42 Yun, Brother., and Paul Hattaway. *The Heavenly Man: The Remarkable True Story of Chinese Christian Brother Yun*, p.154, Monarch Books, 2002.

43 https://www.lucidchart.com/pages/tutorial/venn-diagram (accessed 8/29/2022)

44 This is not an exhaustive list of how God communicates his presence to us, simply the three we have been exploring throughout this work.

45 https://www.history.com/this-day-in-history/earth-quakes-wreak-havoc-in-armenia (accessed 8/29/2022)

46 https://nccb.co.za/wp-content/uploads/2021/06/Spiritual-Formation-Workbook.pdf (accessed 8/29/2022)